THE RHINO SPIRIT

by JAN RUHE

Dedicated to all those with the Rhino Spirit, and you know who you are!

The Rhino Spirit

Copyright © 2003 by Jan Ruhe

Every effort has been made to locate the copyright owner of material in this book. Omission brought to our attention will be corrected in subsequent editions.

This book contains Jan Ruhe's opinions and personal experiences. Her opinions do not necessarily reflect those of her companies, or any persons living or dead unless directly stated.

Cover design by David Anselmo.

ISBN 0-9702667-4-X
LCCN 2003103422

Copyright © 2003 by Jan Ruhe
Published by Proteus Press
300 Puppy Smith, Suite 205-290, Aspen, CO 81611
proteuspress@starband.net
tel. 970-927-9380
fax 970-927-0112
www.janruhe.com

THE RHINO SPIRIT

Introduction

Have you had enough of not getting what you want in life? Is it time to have a better life? A more satisfying, exciting, productive, abundant, prosperous life? Want better relationships? Want to increase the odds that you will be extremely successful? Then get the *Rhino Spirit*. The Rhino has an extremely thick skin. In life, you will have situations and challenges that will toughen you up to be able to better handle life. Just like the skin of the Rhino. Rhinos are rare. To see the Rhino in the bush is an awesome experience. Not many people have the opportunity in their lifetime to see the Rhino in the wild. Once you do, your spirit is changed forever for the better. The Rhino is a fabulous teacher, if we pay attention to it. We can learn a lot from the Rhino. The Rhino protects itself and charges forward massively daily. Everything the Rhino does is massive and bold, just like many want to be like in life. People have libraries full of information on how to be successful. But even after reading the books and listening to tapes or CD's, they aren't successful. Why? Because they don't really understand that what successful people do to get to the top is to charge ahead in spite of all the distractions that come along.

Successful people have had amazing challenges and have worked very hard to achieve their goals. They are unstoppable and tough. They blaze their own trail. They don't slow down. Focus on what you want to have, do and be in life and charge forward to achieve your dreams. If you want to succeed in life, get clear on what you want and charge forward, now! Once you make up your mind to have the *Rhino Spirit* and are clear on what you want, you will not let anyone or any situation distract you from achieving your dreams. You will charge forward during challenging times and you will concentrate all of your energies toward achieving your goals.

Rhinos do not live in the jungle; they live in the bush. They blend in and can hide from attackers. You don't want to attack the Rhino. You will lose. Become a Rhino. When attacked, be the one who can handle it with ease. When you are upset, stop and think of the Rhino spirit and grab this book. When a Rhino is upset, angry, or attacked it charges and gets results. When you are in a challenging situation, think of the Rhino. The Rhino does not run from danger, the Rhino charges forward, unafraid. The Rhino charges forward more than once in a while. If you spend time in the bush, you will see that the Rhino charges ahead. The Rhino will graze for sometime in one place but it's not long before it's on the move. The Rhino is not stopped by the weather. It can weather storms, lightening, hot sun, and chilly nights. It does not complain. It charges forward. Get some massive new goals in life and decide to go forward in a more aggressive way like the Rhino.

Most people just dabble in life. Not those with the *Rhino Spirit*. The Rhino is not complacent or lazy. Wake up from now on every morning and be like a Rhino! Decide you want to live the life of excitement and adventure in the bush of life! Let your life be full of experiences, don't settle for mediocrity. Have the *Rhino Spirit*. Be careful with whom you spend your time. Rhinos hang out with Rhinos. You never see a Rhino hanging out around cows. Keep charging forward in life and the other Rhinos will find you and want to hang out with you too. You can succeed beyond your wildest expectations at any goal you set. You can achieve prosperity and abundance in your life if you will just have the spirit of the Rhino! Forge ahead with all you have. Charge forward! The Rhino never asks for permission to succeed. The Rhino makes decisions and takes action! There will be critical people who try to slow you down, block your path, invade your privacy, gossip and make up mean things about you. Decide to have the *Rhino Spirit*. Your life will change when you do. Become unstoppable and thick skinned. If someone tries to hurt you, don't even notice it. Pay no attention to them and keep charging forward. Do not let anyone make you angry. Anger is difficult to deal with. When someone hurts you from now on, choose to continue to charge forward in life.

When you are really angry, it's hard to do, but you must have the *Rhino Spirit* to carry on with achieving your goals. Read and study successful people who are living the lifestyle you want. Pay attention to unsuccessful people and run away from them. Find out what books they read, what movies they go to, what they do with their time and don't copy them!

Life is going to bring you interesting, fascinating, life challenges. The more successful you are, the more challenges life seems to bring you to handle to help you to the next level in your life. Have the *Rhino Spirit* and if you are knocked down, bounce back quickly and charge ahead even with more resolve! You can put up with a lot of sadness, a lot of bitterness, a lot of unpleasantness when you have the *Rhino Spirit*. Rhinos don't stay mad for long; they handle their challenges and move forward looking for more food, more experiences throughout their lives. With the *Rhino Spirit,* when you get tired, you are able to pick yourself back up again and press on, not letting up on achieving your goals for one minute. You quit blaming your parents, your past, your ex's, your children, your upbringing, your childhood, your government, your church, your teachers, your education or lack of it, your prejudices, your intolerances and you finally take responsibility for your life.

What changes people from being average to wanting to press onward and upward in life like the Rhino? The Rhino makes a decision. That's all. A true decision to charge! Day after day. Those with the *Rhino Spirit* have belief. Believe you can achieve your dreams and keep charging forward until you reach your destination. Success is there for those who want it badly enough and decide to go after their dreams and visions with incredible focus. It's what gets you up early and keeps you working into the night. It is so rewarding to have the *Rhino Spirit.* Rhinos are exciting to be around. They have a zest for living. They are so excited about life that you will rarely find a Rhino who is not going for greatness. Keep your belief strong. Don't let anyone kill your dream. Keep charging! If you quit charging, it's because you have quit believing. Believe and succeed by keeping the *Rhino Spirit* alive and well!

When you make the decision to succeed and you have the belief, the next step is to work on your attitude. If you want to be a Rhino, you will want it so badly that it consumes you. You will want to conquer your goals so badly that you will not be the same old person you were prior to making the decision. You are like a jet plane taking off with incredible energy and forcefulness.

Don't waste a single moment on anything in life that is not important. If you are going after something that you really want, you will go for it with all of your heart. You don't have time in life to fret or to get into a rut or funk. You must charge forward. You are responsible for your future, your success or your failure. You have what it takes to be a Rhino. Charge excitedly into your future.

Don't dwell on the past. Throw off the chains of defeat and past mistakes. You can't change what happened five minutes ago; you can only aggressively meet your future with great anticipation that you are going to be the most successful person you know. Watch what you put into your mind. Rhinos don't watch TV nor read the news, nor think about what all can go wrong. Those with the *Rhino Spirit* read and listen to information that will help them continue to charge forward. In this book you will find stories, poems, ideas, quotes and more that I have collected. These are the main ones that I have referred to over and over again throughout all the trials and tribulations that I endured.

It was in my most devastating challenging times, that I would refer to what is in this book to get me through to the other side of a painful situation. I wanted to preserve the contents of this book so that you might find comfort in the words right here in your hands. I wanted to share them with everyone in the world. Because I know that if these comforted me, and motivated me to be a Rhino, perhaps I can touch one heart, one life, one person who is going through tough times. And perhaps that one person's life will be turned around, turned on, turned up and turned into a beautiful masterpiece! I don't know where I have found you in the circle of your life but I bet there is a story or quote or poem in this book that will feed your spirit. No more is there indecision, you will get and keep the *Rhino Spirit* and pass it on to people in your life. You will no longer be worried about situations that you have no control over. You are bigger than everyone else in life; you are free of worry because you have decided to charge forward in life. Get active; no longer let the chains of mediocrity hold you back. Have the burning desire to become the person you know you can be. Think Rhino thoughts, take massive action and go forth in life knowing that your dreams can all come true. Every single one of them. The Rhino does not ask to be a leader. The Rhino does not wait for someone to recognize him for being a Rhino. The Rhino doesn't pout, or blame others for its situation. The Rhino doesn't need fur coats, diamonds, or fancy cars to feel significant. The Rhino just IS significant. The Rhino makes decisions. Every decision is his, not anyone else's. Do not wait on someone to declare you a champion, declare it for yourself. Keep charging forward in life. Have the *Rhino Spirit*. It's a small world after all. We are so much more alike than different. Those who decide to have the *Rhino Spirit*, at no matter what age, are those who will enjoy life to the fullest. Charge forth and be the best you can be! Create magical moments the rest of your life. Make your life an unforgettable masterpiece!

Don't be average, be a champion, charge into the future with enthusiasm and excitement like your future depends upon it. Because, Rhino friends, it does. Don't be denied the magical lifestyle of those who have . . .

The Rhino Spirit

THE REWARDING LIFE

For life to be the fullest, sweetest and most rewarding:
Do more than move; **improve.**
Do more than get; **give.**
Do more than regret; **repent.**
Do more than look; **see.**
Do more than sympathize; **help.**
Do more than attend church; **worship.**
Do more than have children; **rear them.**
Do more than build a house; **make a home.**
Do more than breathe; **live.**
Do more than live; **love.**

They sailed. They sailed. Then spoke the mate:
"This mad sea shows its teeth tonight.
He curls his lip; he lies in wait,
with lifted teeth, as if to bite!
Brave Admiral, say but one good word.
What shall we do when hope is gone?"
The words leapt as a leaping sword,
"Sail on! sail on! and on!"
-Joaquin Miller

"Tis better to be alone than in bad company."
-George Washington

I BARGAINED FOR LIFE

Isn't it strange that princes and kings
And clowns that caper in sawdust rings;
And common folks, like you and me,
All are builders for eternity.
To each is given a book of rules,
A block of stone and a bag of tools;
And each must shape ere time has flown,
A stumbling block or a stepping stone.
I bargained with life for a penny,
And life would pay no more,
However I begged at evening
When I counted my scanty store.
For life is a just employer,
He gives you what you ask,
But once you have set the wages,
Why, you must bear the task.
I worked for a menial's hire,
Only to learn, dismayed,
That any wage I had asked of life,
Life would have willingly paid.

THE CLIMB

"The small boy heard the mountain speak

There are secrets on my highest peak

But beware, my boy, the passing of time

Wait not too long to start the climb.

So quickly come and go the years

And young man stands below with fears

Come on, come on, the mountain cussed

Time presses on: oh climb, you must.

Now he is busied in middle-age prime

And maybe tomorrow he'll take the climb

Now is too soon; it's raining today

Gone, all gone, years are eaten away.

An old man looks up, still feeling the lure

Yet he'll suffer the pain, not climb for the cure

The hair is white; the step is slow

And it's safer and warmer to stay here below.

So all too soon the secrets are buried

Along with him and regrets he carried

And it's not for loss of secrets he'd cried

But rather because he'd never tried."

-Phyllis Trussler

ATTITUDE

"The longer I live, the more I realize the impact of attitude on life. Attitude, to me, is more important than the past, than education, than money, than circumstances, than failures, than successes, than what other people think or say or do. It is more important than appearance, giftedness or skill. It will make or break a company, a church, or a home.
The remarkable thing is, we have a choice every day regarding the attitude that we will embrace for that day. We cannot change our past, we cannot change the inevitable. The only thing we can do is play on the one string we have, and that is our attitude.
I am convinced that life is 10% what happens to me, and 90% how I react to it. And so it is with you....
we are in charge of our attitudes."
-Charles Swindoll

Let your dreams, not your regrets; take command of your life.

Get the Rhino Spirit!

Be motivated from within. Don't wait on someone to give you significance.

Make your own path in life!
Be like the Rhino!
Be larger than life!
Make your life an unforgettable masterpiece!
The Rhino doesn't spend time
worrying, it takes action!
Keep charging forward in life!
No one can stop a Rhino,
because the Rhino is unstoppable!

THE MASTER ARCHER

A master archer was in the forest with two students. As both students were notching their arrows, preparing to shoot at a target far off in the distance, the master interrupted them and asked each one to describe what he saw.

The first archer said, *"I see the sky and the clouds above, I see the fields and the grass beyond. I see the different trees of the forest, oak, beech, pine, maple, and I see their branches and leaves. I see the target with it's colored rings. I see..."* The master stopped him mid-sentence and said, *"Put down your bow, my son. You are not ready to shoot today."* And then he questioned the second archer, *"What do you see?"* The student replied, *"Nothing but the goal at the center of the target, Master."* *"Then let your arrow fly,"* the teacher directed. And it did, dead on into the very center of the target.

The difference between the two students' state of mind was their single-minded focus. If you have your focus split too many ways, it will be tough to reach your goals.

BE THE BEST

"If you can't be a pine on the top of the hill
Be a scrub in the valley but be
The best little scrub by the side of the hill.
Be a bush if you can't be a tree.
If you can't be a bush, be a bit of grass
And some highway happier make.
If you can't be a muskie, then just be a bass.
But be the liveliest bass in the lake.
We can't all be Captains; we've got to be the crew.
There is something for all of us.
There is big work to do and there's lesser to do
And the task we must do is the near.
If you can't be a highway, then just be the trail.
If you can't be the sun, be a star.
It isn't by size that you win or you fail,
Be the best of whatever you are."
-Douglas Mallock

**When it looks like you've
exhausted all possibilities,
remember this: you haven't.**

CHOICES

Choose to love-rather than hate.
Choose to smile-rather than frown.
Choose to build-rather than destroy.
Choose to persevere-rather than quit.
Choose to praise-rather than gossip.
Choose to heal-rather than wound.
Choose to give-rather than grasp.
Choose to act-rather than delay.
Choose to forgive-rather than curse.
Choose to get fired up-rather than playing it safe.
Choose an life of abundance-rather than that of the average person.
Choose a life of prosperity-take the words: *"little, budget, practical"* and *"I can't afford it"* out of your vocabulary.
Choose to shower the people you love with love-rather than being so busy that you don't take the time to give love starting at home.

W.O.W. = Wonder of Wonders!

CONFUCIUS SAYS

What you do not wish done to yourself, do not do to others.

The great Chou Dynasty was beginning to topple. The feudal system was in chaos and crumbling. There was civil strife and in China, the barons that had emerged as independent states were at war with each other. They struggled to hold onto their power and to their lands and to their people. The Emperor's power had dwindled to nothing. Moral and political chaos was spreading quickly. Widespread confusion and unrest, cruelty, oppression and devastating times were happening rapidly. For every lord who lived in opulence, there were thousands who lived on the edge of starvation. They were humble, though, and endured their servitude and their suffering, with no possible solutions in sight. Murder, pillage, invasion, were commonplace in all of the districts. The very civilization of China was threatened; and the wisest minds, sensing danger, came together to discuss ways to bring peace, order, and harmony once again to their precious, ancient land.

In the state of Lu, in those terrible times, there lived a young man who felt to the extreme the suffering of the people. He knew there was an urgent need for a rationalized social order, and for a system of ethics and morality to guide the tender relationships of the humans of the day. Out of the needs and challenges of his times, this young man was to create a philosophy that remains a vital and living force even today. In our times, today, he made a difference, twenty-five hundred years later. The young man was Ch'iu, of the clan of K'ung. Later he was called K'ung Fu-tse, which means *"the philosopher."* The world today knows him as Confucius.

The story goes that Confucius was born a descendent of noblemen but that is not the truth. Actually, he was born into a poor family. His early years of life are not known, but we do know that even at the age of fifteen he grew up and became interested in the history and literature of his country. He then became a student of the writings of the ancient sages.

China had endured as a great nation for fifteen hundred years. Confucius was convinced that in the rules and precepts of the sages was to be found the guidance now so desperately needed throughout China. He was too close to his own generation to have full knowledge of what was happening. He sensed, as many others did, that China was departing from its ancient moorings. He knew that it's literature and traditions were in danger of perishing through the anarchy into which the kingdom was struggling. He knew that the best way he could help the people and the nation was to discover and salvage the records of antiquity, bring them up to date, interpret and explain their meaning and put them into a practical system of ethics and morals for his time.

It was this goal, his vision in his mind that he established, when he was twenty-two, to teach the history and literature of China. He wanted to share what he had learned about the simple but enduring virtues and values on which the civilization of China was founded. Students began to flock to him from every corner of China, eager to have some reason to live for, some replenishing philosophy. When two young scions of one of the principal houses of Lu joined the growing throng of his disciples, his reputation as a teacher and Master began to grow and spread throughout China.

He had great people skills and because of his wisdom, he was appointed superintendent of the ranges and herds. At this time, this gave him an opportunity to try out one of the most important precepts he had been teaching at his school that he had learned from the sages:

What you do not wish done to yourself, do not do to others.

The ranges he worked for belonged to the state and the herders paid taxes for the use of the land. There was continual strife among the owners of the cattle and sheep. They quarreled constantly. The rival herders hated and distrusted each other, continuing to raid and rob each other whenever they could. They killed or confiscated any animal that strayed on, or even near their land. They were mean to each other and passed vicious rumors about each other throughout the land. Confucius called a meeting of all the herders and spoke to them seriously for a long time. He spoke, not as the usual official in power or overseer, but as a friend, with kindness and understanding. This was totally new; and the herders paid attention, and listened in amazement. And here are some of the wise things Confucius told them: The rule of life is to be found within yourself. Ask yourself constantly:

"What is the right thing to do?"

Beware of ever doing that which you are likely, sooner or later, to repent of having done. It is better to live in peace than in bitterness and strife. It is better to believe in your neighbors than to fear and distrust them. The superior man does not wrangle. He is firm but not quarrelsome. He is sociable but not clannish. The superior man sets a good example to his neighbors. He is considerate of their feelings and their property. Consideration for others is the basis of a good life, a good society. Feel kindly toward everyone. Be friendly and pleasant among yourselves. Be generous and fair.

The wisest value he taught the herders that day was the maxim he was to repeat over and over again throughout his long life and that was to become inseparably associated with his name and his philosophy.

What you do not wish done to yourself, do not do to others.

The herders listened carefully to Confucius and were in total awe by what he said. They returned to their homes and repeated his words to their families. And the strife and turmoil ceased; and the sheep and cattle multiplied; and there was peace on the ranges for the first time in decades. It was an extraordinary display of applied ethics. Confucius was encouraged to continue and expand his wisdom throughout China. His success in ending the strife among the herders enormously increased his influence. His name and fame began to spread rapidly across China. He spent most of the remainder of his life as a student, a scholar and teacher. He wandered from state to state across the country with his disciples, spreading his wisdom wherever he went. He returned to Lu in his old age to collect the ancient traditions and philosophies of his people and his own pithy sayings, for the guidance of future generations.

He died in 479 B.C. at the age of seventy-two. His disciples mourned him as *"the wisest and greatest of mortal men."* They continued to spread his teachings far and wide and the entire Chinese nation began to pay him homage. Among the many posthumous titles conferred upon him were *"The Sage," "The Holy One," "The Master."* Beautiful temples were erected in his memory, and *"Confucianism"* became one of the greatest cults in history. Today, nearly a fourth of the human race love and cherish the memory of Confucius, and look upon his words as sacred writings. Hundreds of thousands of educated Chinese know the five Confucian books by heart and can repeat them word for word. Great masses of people worldwide, even among the most illiterate, live by Confucian teachings as their only religion, their only moral and ethical influence. For twenty-five centuries the teachings of Confucius have remained one of the world's strongest moral forces. At the vital core of his philosophy is the simple, basic rule he taught the warring herdsmen so many years ago:

What you do not wish done to yourself, do not do to others.

Confucius was neither the first nor the last to teach this important social principle and value. It is one of the oldest and most enduring rules of human relationship and behavior. Zoroaster taught it in Persia several hundred years before Confucius. Jesus preached it in Judea five hundred years after Confucius, changing it to the familiar and inspiring Golden Rule of Christianity:

Do unto others, as you would have others do unto you.

Confucius made it the basic principle of his entire philosophy, the most important single rule of life. He preached it tirelessly; his disciples passed it on from one generation to the next; it helped shape the character and destiny of the entire Chinese nation. Though it may not belong to Confucius alone, it was at the root of all his teachings and through his influence has been the guiding principle of countless millions of people since.

From the Analects of Confucius: Tsu-kung asked, saying: "*Is there any one maxim which may serve as a rule of practice for the whole of one's life?*" The Master replied: "*Is not the maxim of charity such?*"

The moral of the story:
What you do not wish done to yourself,
do not do to others.

"All things whatsoever ye would that men should do to you, do ye even so to them: for this is the law and the prophets."
-Matthew 7:12

"He that does good to another does good also to himself, not only in the consequence but in the very act. For the consciousness of well doing is in itself ample reward."

-Seneca

"Deal with others as thou wouldst thyself be dealt by. Do nothing to thy neighbor which thou wouldst not have him do to thee hereafter."
-The Mahabharata

"The duty of man is plain and simple, and consists of two points, his duty to God, which every man must feel; and, with respect to his neighbor, to do as he would be done by."

-Thomas Paine

"It is one of the most beautiful compensations of this life that no man can sincerely try to help another without helping himself."

-Ralph Waldo Emerson

KEY TO HAPPINESS=
DO UNTO OTHERS AS YOU WOULD
HAVE THEM DO UNTO YOU

DO IT ANYWAY

People are illogical, unreasonable,
and self centered.
Love them anyway.
If you do good, people will accuse
you of selfish ulterior motives.
Do good anyway.
If you are successful,
you win false friends and true enemies.
Succeed anyway.
The good you do today will be forgotten tomorrow.
Do good anyway.
Honesty and frankness make you vulnerable.
Be honest and frank anyway.
The biggest men with the biggest ideas can be shot
down by the smallest men with the smallest minds.
Think big anyway.
People favor underdogs but follow only top dogs.
Fight for a few underdogs anyway.
What you spend years building
may be destroyed overnight.
Build anyway.
People really need help,
but may attack you if you do help them.
Help them anyway.
Give the world the best you have and
you'll get kicked in the teeth.
Give the world the best you have anyway.

DON'T GROW OLD

If you have left your dreams behind,
If hope is lost. If you no longer look ahead,
If your ambitious fires are dead.
Then you are old.
But if from life you take the best
And if in life you keep the jest,
If love you hold,
No matter how the years go by,
No matter how the birthdays fly,
You are not old.

GO FOR IT

Go for it! *You might make it!*
Go for it! *It might happen!*
Go for it! *Somebody might be helped by it!*
Go for it! *You might rise from poverty to prosperity!*
Go for it! *If you prosper, you might be able to help
the poor!*
Go for it! *Someday, somebody will come to you and say,
"Thank you!"*

Let your hopes, not your hurts, ...
shape your future.

MANY PATHS

"There is a law that rules, binding to all - even fools.
From the first cell, to the last breath.
From conception, to the point of death.
It's the inner voice: **The Law of Choice.**
We always rise or fall. We cannot stay or stall.
There are many paths to take, many high and low.
And it is up to you to choose, just which way to go.
Some folks drift endlessly, scattered to and fro,
Some know their way, and for others are the show.
What would you do if you could not fail?
Where would you go if you could set any sail?
Episode to adventure, crisscrossing the worlds,
With each decision your Destiny unfurls.
The choice is ever ours that much we know.
To choose the path for our spirit to grow.
Who will ride the waves of chance?
What will you decide?"
-David Wolfe

I WILL PERSIST

"The prizes of life are at the end of each journey, not
near the beginning; and it is not given to me to know
how many steps are necessary in order to reach my
goal. Failure I may still encounter at the thousandth
step, yet success hides behind the next bend in the road.
Never will I know how close it lies unless I turn the
corner...I will persist until I succeed."
-Og Mandino

GREAT TIME TO BE ALIVE

We live in the greatest age that has ever been known in the history of the world. Our forefathers lived on a flat, stationary earth, plowed their ground with a wooden stick. We live today on an earth of power steering and jet propulsion. We live in freedom. With the age of the internet more knowledge than ever before has been released to the world. We live in a world of intelligence. Contrast that to the time people lived in ignorance, superstition and raw uncertainly of the dark ages, who survived the great stock market crash. We live in a day when the knowledge of medicine gives us strong bodies and clear minds. If you had lived 2,000 years ago, your life expectancy at birth would have been 19 years. If you had lived in George Washington's day, in America, it would have been 35 years. But a baby born today in an American hospital has a life expectancy of nearly 75 years. We live in a day in which pain has largely been eliminated. How would you like to have had a tooth pulled or an operation performed, using the methods of 100 years ago. Typewriters are in the past, correction tape is in the past, the day of a phone with a cord on it is in the past. Today you have the ability to become a legend in your own time.

When you get discouraged ask yourself these questions:

- **When would I rather live than now?**
- **Where would I rather live than in a FREE country?**
- **Who would I rather be than who I am?**
- **Is it time to change me?**

I AM RESOLVED

To allow no one nor any situation to disturb
my peace of mind.
To be: a true friend; true to myself; to be kind;
and to count my blessings.
To forget the past mistakes and press on to
greater achievements.
To inspire others by my example; and to keep a
gratitude attitude.
To keep moving forward and upward;
To live life to the fullest and not be afraid
of making commitments.
To make my work a joy; and to risk losing self-control.
To not expect any kindness to be returned
for kindness I give.
To put first things first.
To smile more.
To spend so much time improving myself that I have
no time for criticism of others.
To stand for what is right.
To take every disappointment as a stimulant.
To think the best, work for it and expect it.
After all . . .

Today's accomplishments were

yesterday's impossibilities.

THE UNCOMMON WOMAN

I do not choose to be a common woman.
It is my right to be uncommon since I can.
I seek opportunity, not security.
I do not wish to be a kept citizen, cowed
and deluded by having the government to look after me.
I want to take the calculated risk to dream and to build,
to fail and to succeed.
I refuse to barter incentive for a dole.
I prefer the challenges of life to dole.
I prefer the challenges of life to the guaranteed
existence.
The thrill of fulfillment instead of a stale utopia.
I will not trade freedom for beneficence,
nor my dignity for a handout.
I will never cower before any Master,
nor bend to any threat.
It is my heritage to stand erect, proud and unafraid.
To think and act for myself and my children.
To enjoy the benefits of my creations and to face the
world boldly and to say:

*This I have chosen, I worked hard
and have achieved my dreams.*

I am proud to be a woman.

*I will work harder on myself
than on my job. I will not settle,
I will seek the heights.*

THE LION STORY

On a trip to South Africa, I visited the Entabanie, (means in Zulu *"place in the mountains"*) a beautiful private game resort. Every morning and evening we would go on Game Drives to view the animals. One evening we watched a female and male lion just quietly resting right next to each other. If was absolutely beautiful to see them calm, loving on each other. It's so incredible to see the animals in the wild and not in a zoo or on a TV program or in the movies, but alive right in front of you! We waited and at sunset, they stood, beautifully, majestically, the mighty king of the jungle. They blinked their eyes, stretched, yawned, and appeared to be enjoying the good life without having to work for it.

The lion sleeps, wanders, waits and then hunts. When the sun sinks beneath the horizon, normally in the twilight, the lions begin to hunt. Like a dynamo that has suddenly been switched on, big time, the lion goes to work to earn its dinner. It runs like mad, racing across the land, to catch an animal and eats until its belly is full. Most of the time it MISSES it's target and is totally out of energy, it takes a short rest and then begins the hunt again, never giving up and waiting on someone or some event to help it become successful. It's up to the lion. The lion's natural success faculty triggers action designed to get FULL and stay fulfilled. Instinct lets the lion know when it can relax and enjoy the sun and when it needs to act on the opportunities of the moment to satisfy it's needs. While we were in the area of the lions that night, the guide put a spotlight onto the lions and we watched the lion hunt. The lion was not at all bothered by us, the lion didn't whine or moan or roar at us, it went AFTER what it wanted, food. It was an awesome lesson in being driven to survive. When I think back about my career and being a single mother for several years, although I had many struggles, I am thankful for them because out of those struggles I got clear on the fact that success was up to me and that my children and I would survive! No matter what.

Humans are oriented toward satisfying basic needs for preserving life. The success process drives us far beyond primary needs. It's in our nature to be striving to be achieving goals; our degree of happiness and self esteem is usually at its greatest when we are in active, determined pursuit. Step by step, the drive toward a predetermined goal, the feeling of accomplishment will grow. Take a look at your self image. Financial stability comes to those who know their own strengths and weaknesses. When you cash in on your personal strengths that will eventually mean more money in the bank.

The moral of the story:

"Fuel your success engine with the determination of the lion. Cast off your doubts about tomorrow. Throw off those limiting beliefs. You can make your life whatever you wish it to be, it's up to you. After all, you have the Rhino Spirit!"
-Jan Ruhe

EVERY MORNING IN
AFRICA,
A GAZELLE WAKES UP.
IT KNOWS IT MUST RUN
FASTER THAN THE
FASTEST LION OR IT WILL
BE KILLED . . .
EVERY MORNING A LION
WAKES UP.
IT KNOWS IT MUST
OUTRUN THE SLOWEST
GAZELLE OR IT WILL
STARVE TO DEATH. IT
DOESN'T MATTER
WHETHER YOU ARE A LION
OR A GAZELLE
WHEN THE SUN
COMES UP. . . .
YOU'D BETTER BE
RUNNING.

THE KING AND HIS HAWK

Genghis Khan was a great King and warrior. He led his army into China and Persia, and he conquered many lands. In every country, people talked about his daring deeds; and they said that since Alexander the Great there had been no king like him. One morning when he was home from the wars, he rode out into the woods to hunt. Many of his friends were with him. They rode out cheerfully, carrying their bows and arrows. Behind them came the servants with the hounds. It was a merry hunting party. The woods rang with their shouts and laughter. They expected to carry much game home in the evening.

On the King's wrist sat his favorite hawk that was trained to hunt. At a word from their masters they would fly high up into the air, and look around for prey. If they chanced to see a deer or a rabbit, they would swoop down upon it swift as any arrow. All day long Genghis Khan and his huntsmen rode through the woods. But they did not find as much game as they expected. Toward evening they started for home. The King had often ridden through the woods, and he knew all the paths. So while the rest of the party took the nearest way, he went by a longer road through a valley between two mountains. The day had been warm, and the king was very thirsty. His pet hawk had left his wrist and flown away. It would be sure to find its way home. The king rode slowly along. He had once seen a spring of clear water near this pathway. If he could only find it now! But the hot days of summer had dried up all the mountain brooks. At last, he saw some water trickling down over the edge of a rock. He knew that there was a spring farther up. In the wet season, a swift stream of water always poured down here; but now it came only one drop at a time. The king jumped from his horse. He took a little silver cup from his hunting bag and held it so as to catch the slowly falling drops. It took a long time to fill the cup; and the king was so thirsty that he could hardly wait. At last it was nearly full. He put the cup to his lips, and was about to drink.

All at once there was a whirring sound in the air, and the cup was knocked from his hands. The water was all spilled upon the ground. The king looked up to see who had done this thing. It was his pet hawk. The hawk flew back and forth a few times, and then alighted among the rocks by the spring. The king picked up the cup, and again held it to catch the trickling drops. This time he did not wait so long. When the cup was half full, he lifted it toward his mouth. But before it had touched his lips, the hawk swooped down again, and knocked it from his hands. And now the king began to grow angry. He tried again; and for the third time the hawk kept him from drinking. The king was now very angry indeed. *"How do you dare to act so?"* he cried. *"If I had you in my hands, I would wring your neck!"*

Then he filled the cup again. But before he tried to drink, he drew his sword. *"Now, Sir Hawk,"* he said, *"this is the last time."* He had hardly spoken, before the hawk swooped down and knocked the cup from his hand. But the king was looking for this. With a quick sweep of the sword he struck the bird as it passed. The next moment the poor hawk lay bleeding and dying at its master's feet. *"That is what you get for your pains,"* said Genghis Khan. But when he looked for his cup he found that it had fallen between two rocks, where he could not reach it. *"Now, finally, I will have a drink from that spring,"* he said to himself.

With that he began to climb the steep bank to the place from which the water trickled. It was hard work, and the higher he climbed, the thirstier he became. Finally he reached the place. There indeed was a pool of water; but what was that lying in the pool, and almost filling it? It was a huge, dead snake of the most poisonous kind. The king stopped. He completely forgot his thirst. He thought only of the poor dead bird, his pet hawk lying on the ground below him. *"The hawk saved my life!"* he cried; *"and how did I repay him? He was my best friend, and I have killed him."* He clambered down the bank sadly and so upset with himself. He took the bird up gently, and laid it in his hunting bag. Then he mounted his horse and rode swiftly home. He said to himself, *"I have learned a sad valuable lesson to-day; and that is, never to do anything in anger, someone might be trying to save my life or change my life for the better.*

The moral of the story:
I must first seek to understand the message before I react. I must not assume.

MARCO POLO

Marco Polo was the merchant from Venice who opened the very first trade routes from China to Europe. His story teaches us a lesson in the art of persuading people to get what you want from life. He was one of history's greatest salesmen and a master in the art of getting people to do what he wanted done. People wanted to do things for him. They considered it a favor to be allowed to give him things. How did Marco Polo do this? By the simple knack of making people like him. Today children still play the Marco Polo game in swimming pools. Each child shuts their eyes and the leader yells Marco and the other children try to not get caught have to yell Polo and swim off to another location to try to not be caught. If they are caught, then the game starts over and the one who is caught becomes Marco Polo. And, if the child becomes Marco Polo, the consequence is a privilege, not a horror.

Marco's father, Nicolo and uncle, Maffeo, were experienced businessmen. For years they were prosperous merchants in the city of Venice. They knew how to judge fabrics, what to buy, and how much they could afford to pay for it. Nicolo Polo was worried about his son Marco. Marco didn't seem to take an interest in business trends, facts and figures. Marco just loved people. He mixed and mingled with the crowds. He liked to ride up and down the canals of Venice in a gondola and serenade the beautiful girls who waved at him from their balconies. He was carefree and happy and wherever he went he made people laugh and forget their troubles. However, Marco did have a business head on his shoulders and his father knew this. He used to say, *"The boy will either be a famous businessman or a famous poet."* So when Nicolo and Maffeo were ready to make their second business voyage to China, they took Marco along. China was a land of great riches, priceless art, fine fabrics and all sorts of great items that would bring a big price in Venice. Nicolo and Maffeo had only been partly successful in selling themselves to the great Kublai Kahn. They hoped Marco would turn out to be a great trader and thought if they took him to China he would get his mind on the family business. The Polos took six years to make the trip from Venice to the kingdom of Kublai Kahn. The entire six years the father and uncle taught Marco on how to bargain, how to negotiate and how to do business with the great Kublai Kahn.

When they arrived they anticipated that Marco would call a business conference and try to give the Khan a presentation on why he should trade with them. However, that did not happen. Not at all. Marco had not changed a bit. He still was more interested in people than in statistics. Instead of making a presentation to Khan to convert the great leader to European ways of thinking, he was more interested in learning from the Khan the oriental way of life. And he set out to make friends with Kublai Khan and he did just that. Marco was such an interesting person to have around that the Khan had him move into a spare room in his palace. Weeks went by and Marco didn't even mention business. Instead, he admired the women in Khan's harem, dined with the Khan and swapped stories and jokes with him. Nicolo and Maffeo were getting worried by the day. Why wouldn't Marco get to business? Why didn't he get busy and begin to make his presentation to Khan. They begin to think that all their hopes and dreams in Marco were for naught. He was getting nowhere. But Marco had a plan. The Khan liked Marco so much that he began to heap gifts upon him. He made him a member of his Imperial Council and appointed him his personal representative when Marco wanted to visit other parts of China and learn more of the ways of this *"land of the unknown."* He even tried to make him a Prince and give him a kingdom of his own!

When they returned to Europe, they had precious treasures that the Khan had given to Marco, because he wanted to. Marco had made the Khan desire to do something for the Polos. Marco had become a wonderful companion and sincere friend of the Khan. Marco proved to be the best businessman by not being a businessman. Today, we cannot afford to take up weeks and months of time becoming best friends with everyone with which we wish to do business. In our day and age conditions have changed, but people haven't. We still like to do things for the people we like. When we really like a person, we tend to minimize his mistakes and shortcomings and magnify his good points. When we dislike a person, just the opposite is true. Nothing he nor she does pleases us. Work on making friends with people. Learn from them. Don't be in such a hurry to get the sale.

The moral of the story:
*Make people like you, sell yourself
and build relationships.*

Nothing great ever happens on the OK level.

BE UNSTOPPABLE!

KEEP CHARGING FORWARD

HAVE RHINO COURAGE

The experiences I accumulated during 28 years of association with the Navy were very helpful in determining decisions I made. There will be times during your career that you will want to take a stand on a certain principle or choose to take a certain course of action, while doing so maybe you would like others to follow you.

During the Vietnam war, I was assigned to a Guided Missile Destroyer, as a helicopter pilot. I had a crew of three to lead into combat. Combat in the Navy, at that time, was voluntary so I had to exhibit leadership that would encourage the crew to fly with me in the most dangerous of missions. What I discovered was not from books or training sessions but from listening to the crewmen tell stories about *"such and such"* pilot. *"He was a great pilot, he could make the plane do anything he wanted, I'd fly with him anytime, anywhere!"* Wow! I listened and paid attention to all those positive comments. I wanted my crew to feel that way about me. I set a goal to be the best, the most proficient helicopter pilot the Navy ever had. As I was reaching my proficiency goal, the great confidence I had in my abilities grew and that created my courage. I leapt at the chance to fly a combat mission into Viet Nam. And my crew followed me. We flew 46 missions over North Viet Nam during two tours and we were awarded many medals for our efforts. In combat people will follow the leader who is proficient and courageous and one who can make life or death decisions. Someone with the spirit of a Rhino. Tough. My recommendation is to always face your fears and become proficient in your career. Be courageous, think big, make powerful decisions and people will emulate what you show and they too will grow and be the best. Have the spirit of the Rhino. After being in combat, leadership in the Navy takes on a different style. Leadership through the *"structure"* becomes the name of the game. The structure is much like a pyramid. The Admiral is at the top; the enlisted man is at the bottom. Nothing else is required to be a leader but that you're at the top of someone else. *"I'm an officer-you're an enlisted man-do what I say-now!"*

Do you have anyone in your life who tries to *"pull rank?"* They say something like; *"I've been with this company for ten years so let me tell you what to do!"* The challenge is, they haven't done anything with their business. They set themselves up to be trainers of everyone in the *"how-to"* and the information they teach gets the company or their business absolutely nowhere.

In the Navy, being given orders by superiors that I felt were incompetents who had reached their peak, got old. So I left active duty with the Navy and went into the Naval Reserves. The Naval Reserve was run by Officers who were business or professional men the rest of the month. I was in the Navy prior to the introduction of many women, hence my use of the word men when referring to the Navy. The enlisted men were civilians the rest of the month and some even made more money than their Officers. Leadership by virtue of the structure got you nowhere in the Reserves. There is structure in the Reserves because you were after all a military unit; but there is also the *"consideration"* style of leading. Consideration is a style of leadership where you value your men and are considerate of their needs. You, the leader make them feel valued. You train them to be responsible, to take the initiative and accomplish goals without constant supervision. When your unit earns the "E" for excellence award it is earned by each person doing his part toward the goal. The leader does not take the credit for reaching the goal. It's a team goal. Each part of the team is valued.

My last Commanding Officer in the Reserves owned his own company in Arkansas and would fly in the Friday night before our weekend in his private plane. He met with us at our first formation on Saturday morning, had a cup of coffee with us, ask us if we needed him for anything, and we'd say "*no.*" We'd see him at the Officer's Club Saturday evening and then the next time we'd see him was on Sunday at our last formation. It was even rumored that he may be golfing during the weekend. As the Executive Officer, I felt it my duty to inquire of our CO about his "*style*" of leadership. He shared with me the greatest style of leadership yet. Train your followers to lead themselves. To become the best they can be, champions! There is a lot to learn from the discipline of the military. The highest rank in the Navy is a 4-Star Admiral. There are only a few. There is only one position even above the 4-Star Admiral and that is the Chief of Naval Operations who reports to the President of the United States. The President of the United States is the Commander in Chief of the United States military.

The moral of the story:

"Pay attention to the military champions, they have worked hard to get to the top. They are tough-minded individuals. They have the Rhino Spirit and they have Rhino Courage."

-Commander William James Ruhe, Jr.

(USNR-RET.)

NOTHING STOPS THE RHINO

How sweet it is to stand on the edge of tomorrow.

PRESS ON

Nothing in the world can take the place of persistence. Talent will not; nothing is more common than unsuccessful men with talent. Genius will not; unrewarded genius is almost a proverb. Education alone will not; the world is full of educated derelicts. Persistence and determination alone are omnipotent.

IT'S UP TO YOU

Dear Rhino,

The population of the United States is approximately 200 million. There are 72 million people over the age of 65, which leaves 128 million people to work. Then there are 75 million people under the age of 21, which leaves 53 million people to work. Then there are 24 million people employed by the federal government, which leaves 29 million people to work. There are 13 million people in the US armed forces, which leaves 16 million to do the work. Deduct 14,650 million and that is the number employed by the state and local governments and the 520 thousand in hospitals and you have 715 thousand people left to work. Now out of these 715 thousand subtract 462 thousand bums, homeless and vagrants who won't work. So that leaves 253 thousand. Now it might interest you to know that there are 252,999 people in jail. So that just leaves 2 people to carry the load. That's you and I and I'm going on vacation tomorrow.

Love,
Susie Creamcheese

GET IN THE GAME OF LIFE

LASTING WEALTH

"Wealth is not the things we own. A stately house upon a hill, paintings, rugs and tapestries, servants taught to do one's will. In luxury, a man may dwell as lonely as in a prison cell. Wealth is not a plenteous purse, the bonds that one has stored away, a boastful balance in a bank, nor jeweled bobbles that fools display. Things that really gratify are things that money cannot buy. Wealth is health and a cheerful heart, an ear that hears the robin's song, a mind content, some treasured friends and fragrant memories lingering on. Living is an inward art, all lasting, wealth is in the heart."

-Longfellow

You will never win ...
if you never begin

LIVE LIFE

The quality of my life today is up to me
and no one else.
I can make good of it or I can waste it.
Since it will never come again,
I will make the best of it.
I will make this day one of success
instead of failure,
joy rather than sorrow, love rather than hate.
Satisfaction rather than frustration,
laughter rather than tears.
The choice is mine.
I will live creatively, enthusiastically
and proudly. I will live this day to the fullest.

Storms always lose to the sun

CHOOSE TO LIVE WITH THE RHINO SPIRIT

THE SIDE OF THE ROAD

Sam Foss loved to take long walks. He had wandered a bit too far today in the hot sun, lost in his thoughts and suddenly he realized how hot and tired he was. The big tree at the side of the road looked tempting and he stopped to rest in its shade. There was a small sign on the tree, and he read it with surprise and pleasure. The sign said: *"There is a good spring inside the fence. Come and drink if you are thirsty."* Foss climbed over the fence, found the spring, and gratefully drank his fill of the cool water. Then he noticed a bench near the spring, and tacked to the bench another sign. He went over to it and read: *"Sit down and rest awhile if you are tired."* Now thoroughly excited he went to a barrel of apples near by and saw that amazingly here too was another sign! *"If you like apples, just help yourself,"* he read. He accepted the invitation, picked out a plump red apple and looked up to discover and elderly man watching him with interest.

"Hi there!" Foss said, *"Is this your property?"* *"Yes,"* the old man answered. *"And I am glad you stopped by."* *"Tell me about all of these signs,"* said Foss. The old man began to speak. *"The water was going to waste; the bench was gathering dust in the attic; the apples were more than we could use. My wife and I thought it would be neighborly to offer tired, thirsty passers-by a place to rest and refresh themselves. So we brought down the bench and put up the signs, and made a host of fine new friends!"* *"You must like people,"* Foss said. *"Of course we do,"* the old man answered. *"Don't you?"*

All the way home Sam Foss kept thinking of a line from Homer's Iliad: *"He was a friend of man and lived in a house by the side of the road.*" How perfectly that described the kindly old man he had met, living in his house by the side of the road, eagerly sharing his water and the comfort of his grounds, being a friend to strangers who passed by. All of a sudden he began a poem in his mind about friendship.

The House By the Side of the Road

"There are hermit souls that live withdrawn
In the place of their self-content;
There are souls like stars, that dwell apart,
In a fellowless firmament;
There are pioneer souls that blaze their paths
Where highways never ran-
But let me live by the side of the road
And be a friend to man.
Let me live in a house by the side of the road,
Where the race of men go by-
The men who are good and the men who are bad,
As good and as bad as I.
I would not sit in the scorner's seat,
Or hurl the cynic's ban-
Let me live in a house by the side of the road
And be a friend to man.
I see from my house by the side of the road,
By the side of the highway of life,
The men who pass with the ardor of hope,
The men who are faint with the strife.
But I turn not away from their smiles nor their tears,
Both parts of an infinite plan-
Let me live in a house by the side of the road
And be a friend to man.
I know there are brook-gladdened meadows ahead,
And mountains of wearisome height;
That the road passes on through the long afternoon
And stretches away to the night.

But still I rejoice when the travelers rejoice,
And weep with the strangers that moan,
Nor live in my house by the side of the road
Like a man who dwells alone.
Let me live in my house by the side of the road,
Where the race of men go by-
They are good, they are bad, they are weak,
they are strong,
Wise, foolish-so am I;
Then why should I sit in the scorner's seat,
Or hurl the cynic's ban?
Let me live in my house by the side of the road
And be a friend to man."
-Sam Walter Foss

Sam Walter Foss passed away in 1911. Millions love his poem. Because a poet went walking one hot summer day, and met a kind old man who loved people and loved doing things for people, we have a cherished poem. In the hustle and bustle of your life today, stop for a moment and think of someone else on their path through life.

ADD UP YOUR JOYS AND NEVER COUNT YOUR SORROWS.

HAVE NO MALICE

What started out to be a dull and rainy day in March, 1865 soon changed. The clouds parted, the day cleared and it turned out to be a beautiful day for the President's second inauguration. The streets were packed with people enjoying the festivities. The inauguration platform was on the east front of the United States Capitol. There was a vast sea of humanity, stretching as far as the eye could see, filling the great plaza and flowing out onto the grounds beyond. When the President appeared and took his place on the platform a tremendous roar swept the crowd, loud and prolonged.

Abraham Lincoln had not expected such a greeting and ovation. He had not expected to be re-elected at all. No man in American history had been so hated and reviled. He was bitterly denounced for the past four difficult years of great struggle and suffering, of agony and bloodshed. He had become the leader of the country at a time of grave crisis. He had given his very best efforts to maintain and preserve the Union, the only thing that really mattered. He had been misunderstood, criticized, condemned, humiliated and misquoted both in public and in private, assailed alike by friend and foe. An editorial was written demanding his withdrawal in favor of another candidate, saying: "*Mr. Lincoln is already beaten. He can never be elected.*" His life had been threatened over and over again. Even today though every precaution had been taken, he knew that there were many who feared for his safety.

He had not expected to be elected, not even with the excitement that the Confederacy had been broken and that victory was in sight. With Grant's vise closing on Lee, and Sherman moving up from the south, it was apparent that the war was almost over. He felt no elation, either at the recent victories in the war or his own unexpected amazing victory at the polls. He had an attitude of gratitude for the chance now given him to complete his great task. He harbored no resentments, had no slightest wish for retaliation against those who had cruelly slandered and abused him. He had one goal only: to conciliate the rebellious states and to rebuild the Union he had sworn to preserve. He had the *Rhino Spirit*.

The crowd fell silent as he stepped forward to make his address. The sun, which had been hidden all day, suddenly burst through the clouds and completely flooded the scene with brightness. He spoke slowly and clearly, his voice vibrant and strong with emotion, aware of the great importance of this moment and the potential influence of his words on the entire nation.

"On the occasion corresponding to this four years ago, all thoughts were anxiously directed to an impending civil war...all knew that slavery was, somehow, the cause of the war...neither party expected for the war the magnitude or the duration which it has already attained. Each looked for an easier triumph...both read the same Bible, and pray to the same God; and each invokes His aid against the other...it may seem strange that any men should dare to ask a just God's assistance in wringing their bread from the sweat of other men's faces; but let us judge not, that we be not judged...The Almighty has His own purposes..."

The crowd listened in silence. This was not party language. This was not political phraseology. Lincoln was talking out of the fullness of his heart; to a people and nation he loved, appealing for peace and tolerance, for understanding, for an end to the bitterness and strife.

There was no hint of self-aggrandizement anywhere in his speech, no boasting about his re-election, no praise for the administration and what it had accomplished. The Union was his main theme, his main interest…a strong, united, and an unbroken nation, above all, no malice. The issues involved were too vast to admit of malicious dealing. His aim was to end all feelings of hatred and resentment between North and South, to bind up the nation's wounds, to prevent, in so far as possible, the unhappy aftermath of war. He closed with this passage, which has been called *"the purest gold of human eloquence:"*

"With malice toward none; with charity for all; with firmness in the right, as God gives us to see the light, let us strive on to finish the work we are in; to bind up the nation's wounds; to care for him who shall have borne the battle, and for his widow and his orphan, to do all which may achieve and cherish a just and lasting peace among ourselves and with all nations."

Lincoln's second inaugural address received high contemporary praise. Newspapers declared it the most inspiring speech ever made by an American President. It was declared that it raised high hopes for the future, and many congratulated the President on finding words so eloquent and so adequate to his desire. It was in the closing paragraph of Lincoln's speech that had the greatest impact that stirred the nation and the world. In these few words were condensed the essence of his philosophy, his abiding faith in the nation and its people, his dream of an America in which all were equally free, and in which even the most humble could find peace and happiness. They were words of a man with a *Rhino Spirit*, infinite sympathy and compassion. Though he spoke out of the depth of his own heart, he spoke for millions of others who felt as he did, voicing their hopes and prayers for a lasting peace *"with liberty and justice for all."* It was a speech forever memorable and forever inspiring. The language was simple and there was majesty to it. No President had ever spoken words like these to the American people. This famous closing paragraph was an expression of Lincoln's own values, his courage and integrity, his humility and love for his fellow man. *"With malice toward none, with charity for all."* Lincoln did not believe in harboring bitter feelings, resentments or grudges. He never willingly planted a thorn in any man's bosom, and never did anything through malice or spite.

Few words have had such tremendous and enduring influence on people worldwide. What an outstanding example of the *Rhino Spirit*.

Success without conflict is unrealistic.

NEVER GIVE UP

Lincoln could have given up many times. Because he didn't quit, he became one of the greatest President's in the history of the United States of America. Born into poverty, Lincoln was faced with defeat throughout his life. He lost eight elections, twice failed in business and suffered a nervous breakdown. Here is his track record on his way to the White House:

1831- Failed in business.
1832- Defeated for Legislature.
1833- Second failure in business.
1836- Suffered nervous breakdown.
1838- Defeated for speaker.
1840- Defeated for Elector.
1843- Defeated for Congress.
1848- Defeated for Congress.
1855- Defeated for Senate.
1856- Defeated for Vice President.
1858- Defeated for Senate.
1860- ELECTED PRESIDENT OF THE UNITED STATES.

Capitalize on your crisis.

SEEK THE TRUTH

*"Take constructive action. Strive to achieve the
highest ideals you can conceive, consistent
with good physical and mental health.
Live intelligently in your society.
Abstain from that which will cause
unnecessary injury.
Start from where you are and go to where you
want to be regardless of what you are or
what you have been."*
-Napoleon Hill

In your day to day comments, abandon the
" *if only*" and substitute "*however*"
or "*at least*" or "*next time.*"

MY ROBOT

I have a little Robot that goes around with me;
I tell him what I am thinking, I tell him what I see.
I tell my little Robot all my hopes and fears;
He listens and remembers all my joys
and all my tears.
At first my little Robot followed my command;
but after years of training he's gotten out of hand.
He doesn't care what's right or wrong, or what is
false or true; now…no matter what I try,
he tells me what to do!

Turn your *"shoulds"*
into *"**musts**."*

A MESSAGE FROM MR. LION

This is tale of vicious, senseless animal slayings that guides Rhinos to true wisdom. The story is of a donkey, a lion, and a fox that decided to go out hunting for rabbits. After a pretty good day of hunting, they had collected a large pile of rabbits. The lion said to Mr. Donkey, "*I'd like for you to divide the rabbits fairly among the three of us.*" So, the donkey took the rabbits and made them into three equal piles and said, "*How's that?*" The lion immediately pounced on the donkey and killed him. Then the lion threw all the rabbits on top of the donkey and made one big pile. The lion turned to Mr. Fox and said, "*I'd like for you to divide the rabbits evenly between the two of us.*" The fox walked over to the pile of rabbits and took one little scrawny rabbit for himself and put it in his pile. He left the rest of the rabbits in a large pile and said, "*That pile of rabbits is for you, Mr. Lion.*" The lion said, "*Mr. Fox, where did you learn to divide so evenly?*" And the fox replied, "*The donkey taught me.*"

The moral of the story:

If you can learn from your own mistakes, you are smart. However, if you can learn from others' mistakes

you are wise.

BRUCE AND THE SPIDER

There was once a brave and wise king of Scotland whose name was Robert Bruce. The times in which he lived were wild and rude. The King of England was at war with him, and had led a great army into Scotland to drive him out of the land. He was prepared, determined and had an attitude that he would not be defeated even though his army was much smaller than the great King of England. Many battles were fought. Six times had Bruce led his brave little army against his foes; and six times had his men been beaten, and driven into flight. His tiny army was scattered, and he was forced to hide in the woods and in lonely places in the mountains. He was worried and thought about quitting the battle and giving up. He was almost defeated, but he was determined not to give up.

One rainy day, Bruce lay on the ground under a rude shed, listening to the patter of the raindrops on the roof above him. He was tired and sick at heart, and ready to give up all hope. It seemed to him that there was no use for him to try to do anything more. His little army was scattered through the forest. He began to ponder his future and the future of Scotland, when suddenly he saw a spider over his head, making ready to weave her web. He watched her as she toiled slowly and with great care. Six times she tried to throw her frail thread from one beam to another, and six times it fell short. *"Poor thing!"* said Bruce: *"You, too, know what it is to fail."* But the spider did not lose hope with the sixth failure. With still more care, she made ready to try for the seventh time. Bruce almost forgot his own troubles as he watched her swing herself out upon the slender line. Would she fail again? No! The thread was carried safely to the beam, and fastened there. *"I, too, will try a seventh time!"* cried Bruce.

He arose and took urgent action. He made no excuses; he would not be denied and called his men back together. He told them of his plans, his visions, his hopes and dreams, and sent them out with messages of cheer to his disheartened people. Soon there was an army of brave Scotsmen around him. Another battle was fought and that little band of them defeated the English army! The lesson, which the little creature had taught the king was never forgotten. Don't give up on the sixth try, keep trying. Never give up. It might just work the seventh time!

The moral of the story:

Never Give Up! Press on!

FINDING GOLD

There were many gold diggers who had been digging for gold way up in the mountains. Most had given up, as they didn't think they would ever find any gold. One man kept on going back into the mountains, day after day. All of a sudden, after years of digging for gold, he was up in the mountains early in the day and he suddenly hit gold. Every place he dug, there was gold. More gold than he had ever seen in his life. More gold than he ever expected to see in his whole life! And it was his! He found it, and now he owned it. He started filling his truck up as quickly as he could shovel, carrying the gold. He was a millionaire now! He had been searching and digging for gold for years. Everyone else had given up, discouraged but him. He had believed it was there and he did not give up. Now there it was gleaming, glistening in the sun. He was so excited, he filled up his truck, the front seat, filled it every place except where he needed to get into the truck to drive. But still there was more. He went out of the mountains and called his friend Andy. What do you think that the gold digger said? Do you think that he said, *"Andy, is this a good time for us to talk? Uh, Andy, I might have something that you might be interested in."* No! He said, *"Andy, hurry up, meet me up in the hills where we have been looking for gold! I found it! I want to share it with you, hurry!"*

The moral of the story:
Get excited about what you are doing and share it!

THE GOLD RUSH

There was a man in Northern California, in 1847 that owned a large ranch. He read that gold had been discovered in Southern California, and he sold his ranch to Colonel Sutter and started off to hunt for gold. He was determined to find it and bought all kinds of tools before he started his hunt so he would be prepared. He had a vision of being wealthy and living a fabulous lifestyle when he found the gold. He could not wait to get started. He had a vision, he had tools, and he had determination. He was fired up and ready to make his fortune. Colonel Sutter put a mill on a small stream on that farm. One afternoon his little girl brought some wet sand from the raceway of the mill into the house and placed it before the fire to dry, and as that sand was falling through the girl's fingers a visitor saw the first shining scales of real gold that were ever discovered in California. Think about the man who wanted the gold, who had sold his ranch and gone away, never to return. On his own ranch, the stream was filled with gold! Today, that mine is still not exhausted yet, and that a one-third owner of that farm has been getting during these recent years $100 of gold every 15 minutes of his life, sleeping or waking.

The moral of the story:

There is opportunity all around you even today.
It's right in front of you. You can have everything,
vision, the tools, the determination, a winning attitude
and the Rhino Spirit.

DR. RHINO HAS THE CURE

There was once a kind man, Dr. Rhino who had a gentle spirit. He was always ready to help others and to share with them anything that he had. He gave away so much to the poor that he was always poor himself. One day a poor woman asked Dr. Rhino to go and see her husband, who was sick and could not eat. Dr. Rhino did so. He found that the family was in great need. The man had not worked for a long time. He was not sick, but in distress; and, as for eating, there was no food in the house. "*I will be back this afternoon with some medicine for your husband, meet me in the lobby of the hotel on Main Street,*" said Dr. Rhino to the woman. That afternoon the woman waited and finally Dr. Rhino arrived. He handed her a little paper box that was very heavy. It did not look like how she had ever seen medicine packaged.

"*Here is the medicine,*" he said. "*Use it faithfully, and I think it will do your husband a great deal of good. But don't open the box until you reach home.*"

"*What are the directions for taking it?*" asked the woman. "*You will find them inside of the box,*" he answered. When the woman reached her home, she sat down by her husband's side, and they opened the box. What do you think they found in it? It was full of pieces of money. And on the top were the directions: —

"TO BE TAKEN AS OFTEN AS NECESSITY REQUIRES."

It wasn't long before her husband began to feel better. He had worked all his life and had saved what he could, but not enough. Many people go through life working their hearts out to provide for others. When they stop working, if they have no savings and the money stops coming in and there is no one to provide for them they begin to become ill, not from anything except fear and sadness.

The moral of the story:

Never take anyone for granted. Have the Rhino Spirit and prepare for your future.

Never let a challenge become an excuse.

As life goes on . . . it's a good idea to take a check-up from the neck up from time to time!

INVISIBLE KISSES

We often learn the most from our children. Some time ago, a friend of mine punished his three-year-old daughter for wasting a roll of gold wrapping paper. Money was tight and he became infuriated when the child tried to decorate a box to put under the tree. However, the little girl brought the gift to her father the next morning and said, "*This is for you, Daddy.*" He was embarrassed by his earlier over-reaction, but his anger flared again when he found that the box was empty. He yelled at her, "*Don't you know that when you give someone a present, there's supposed to be something inside of it?*" The little girl looked up at him with tears in her eyes and said, "*Oh Daddy, it's not empty. I blew kisses into the box all for you, Daddy.*" The father put his arm around his little girl, and he begged for her forgiveness. He kept that gold box by his bed for the rest of his life. Whenever he was discouraged, he would take out an imaginary kiss and remember the love of the child who had put it there.

The moral of the story:
Each of us as parents has been given a gold container filled with unconditional love and kisses from our children. There is no more precious possession anyone could hold.

JULIUS CAESAR

Nearly 2,000 years ago lived the greatest warriors of all the Romans, Julius Caesar. He knew how to make men both love, fear and follow him. Ultimately, he was the ruler of Rome. Once when Caesar was passing through a little country village, all the people came out to see him. There were not more than fifty of them led by their mayor, who told each one what to do. These simple people of the village stood by the roadside and watched Caesar pass. The mayor looked very proud and happy; for was he not the ruler of this village? He felt that he was almost as great a man as Caesar himself. Some of the officers who were with Caesar laughed. They said, "*See how that fellow struts at the head of his little flock!*" "*Laugh as you will,*" said Caesar, "*he has reason to be proud. I would rather be the head man of a village than the second man in Rome!*" Another time, Caesar was crossing a narrow sea in a boat. Before he was halfway to the farther shore, a storm overtook him. The wind blew hard; the waves clashed high; the lightning flashed; the thunder rolled. It seemed any minute as though the boat would sink. The captain was in great fright. He had crossed the sea many times, but never in such a storm as this. He trembled with fear; he could not guide the boat; he fell down upon his knees; he moaned, "*All is lost! all is lost!*" Caesar was not afraid. He commanded the man get up and take his oars again and not give in or give up. "*Why should you be afraid?*" he said.

> "*The boat will not be lost; for you have*
> *Caesar on board.*"

THE AGE OF THE GOOF-OFF

Charlie Brower made an interesting speech before the National Sales Executive Club in New York. He pointed out some of the weaknesses that we've developed, even while living in the greatest age of wonders and enlightenment ever known in the world. He said: *"I'm sick and tired of teachers who don't want to teach and preachers who don't want to preach and salesmen who don't like to sell, and workers who won't work. But the thing that makes me the sickest is the leaders who won't lead."*

-Charlie Brower

Even the Rhino takes a well deserved rest now and then.

TAKE RISKS

To laugh is to risk appearing the fool.
To weep is to risk appearing sentimental.
To reach out for another is to risk involvement.
To expose feelings is to risk exposing your true self.
To place your ideas, your dreams before a
crowd is to risk their loss.
To love is to risk not being loved in return.
To live is to risk dying.
To hope is to risk despair.
To try is to risk failure.
But risks must be taken, because the greatest
hazard in life is to risk nothing.
The person, who risks nothing, does nothing,
has nothing and is nothing.
They may avoid suffering and sorrow, but they
cannot learn, feel, change, grow, love, and live.
Chained by their attitudes, they are a slave;
they have forfeited their freedom.

Only a person
who risks is free.

OPPORTUNITY IS RIGHT IN FRONT OF YOU!

Many years ago, a young man from Massachusetts went to study at Yale University and studied mines and mining. They paid him $15 a week during his last year for training students who were behind in their classes in mineralogy, while pursuing his own studies. When he graduated they raised his pay from $15 to $45 dollars and offered him a professorship. He discussed the offer with his mother and said, "*Mother, I won't work for $45 dollars a week. What is $45 a week for a man with a brain like mine! Mother, let's go out west and stake out gold claims and be immensely rich.*" "*Now,*" said his mother, "*it is just as well to be happy as it is to be rich and I don't particularly want to move.*" After much debate, she agreed and they moved to Wisconsin, where he went into the employ of the Superior Copper Mining Company. He went to work for that company at $15 a week again. He was also to have an interest in any mines that he should discover for that company. But he never discovered a mine. He had scarcely gone from the old homestead in Massachusetts before the farmer who had bought the homestead went out to dig potatoes. He was bringing them in a large basket through the front gateway; the ends of the stone wall came so near together at the gate that the basket hugged very tight. So he set the basket on the ground and pulled, first on one side and then on the other side.

The farms in Massachusetts are mostly surrounded by stone walls, and the farmers have to be economical with their gateways in order to have some place to put the stones. That basket hugged so tight there that as he was hauling it through he noticed in the upper stone next to the gate a block of native silver, eight inches square.

The professor of mines and mining and mineralogy, who would not work for $45 a week, when he sold that homestead in Massachusetts, sat right on that stone to make the bargain to sell the homestead! He was brought up there from the time he was a little boy; he had gone back and forth by that piece of silver, rubbed it with his sleeve, and it seemed to say, "*Come now, now, now, here is a hundred thousand dollars. Why not take me?*" But he would not take it. There was no silver in the area of Wisconsin that he had moved to. The riches he was seeking were so close. He was a smart young man; he just missed the opportunity right in front of his eyes for his entire life. There is opportunity for you right before your eyes.

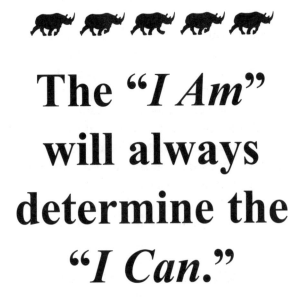

The "*I Am*" will always determine the "*I Can.*"

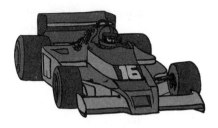

RELEASE YOUR BRAKES!

Believe that dreamers are believers
and the believers are receivers.
Know this truth, that to believe is all it takes.
Just take heart, get past the losers,
never quit, you're among choosers.
Choose that dream; set that goal;
release your brakes!
It takes a special kind of caring,
and a lot of active sharing.
A better you, a better me, that's what it takes.
For success is but a journey
and we all win in this tourney,
Get out of tow; give in; let go;
release your brakes!
Reach for your dream, your heart has spoken.
Full speed ahead, there's no use pokin',
You're a winner, why not stretch for winner's stakes?
Time is not all that you're losin'
For the best is yet for choosin'.
Step on your fears; shift your gears;

release your brakes!

TEACHINGS OF TECUMSEH

April 9, 1809

So live your life that the fear of death can never enter your heart. Trouble no one about his religion; respect yours. Love your life, perfect your life, and beautify all things in your life. Seek to make your life long and of service to your people. Prepare a noble death song for the day when you go over the Great Divide. Always give a word or sign of salute when meeting a passing friend, or even a stranger, if in a lonely place. Show respect to all people, but grovel to none. When you arise in the morning give thanks for the light, for your life and strength. Give thanks for your food and for the joy of living. If you see no reason for giving thanks, the fault lies in yourself. Touch not the poisonous firewater that makes wise ones turn to fools and robs the Spirit of its vision. When your time comes to die be not like those whose hearts are filled with the fear of death, so that when their time comes they weep and pray for a little more time to live their lives over again in a different way. Live your life so that when you sing your death song, you will die like a hero who is going home with no shame to meet the Creator and your family.

Shower the people you love with love

THE AWAKENING

A time comes in your life when you finally get it…when in the midst of all your fears and insanity you stop dead in your tracks and somewhere the voice inside your head cries out-enough! Enough fighting and crying or struggling to hold on. And, like a child quieting down after a blind tantrum, your sobs begin to subside, you shudder once or twice, you blink back your tears, and through a mantel of wet lashes you begin to look at the world through new eyes. **This is your awakening.**

You learn:

-**about love**. Romantic love and familial love. How to love, how much to give in love, when to stop giving and when to walk away.

-**to admit when you are wrong** and to building bridges instead of walls.

-**to be thankful and have a gratitude attitude.**

-**to begin reassessing and redefining** who you are and what you really stand for.

-**to deal with evil** in its most primal state–the ego.

-**to discard the doctrines and values you've outgrown,** or should never have bought into to begin with.

-**to fight for your life** and not to squander it living under a cloud of impending doom.

-**to look at relationships as they really are** and not as you would have them be.

-**to step right through your fears** because you know that whatever happens you can handle it, and to give in to fear is to give away the right to live life on your terms.

-**not to project your needs or your feelings** onto a relationship. You stop working so hard at putting your feelings aside, smoothing things over and ignoring your needs.

-the importance of loving and championing yourself and in the process a sense of new found confidence is born of self-approval.

You learn that:

-alone does not mean lonely.

-anything worth achieving is worth working for, and that wishing for something to happen is different from working toward making it happen.

-fatigue diminishes the spirit and can create doubt and fear. So take more time to rest.

-feelings of entitlement are perfectly OK…and that it is your right to want things and to ask for the things that you want…and that sometimes it is necessary to make demands.

-God isn't punishing you or failing to answer your prayers. It's just life happening.

-in life you get what you believe you deserve…and that much of life truly is a self-fulfilling prophecy.

-in order to achieve success you need direction, discipline and perseverance.

-it is important to open up to different points of view.

-it is time to stop hoping and waiting for something to change or for happiness, safety and security to come galloping over the next horizon.

-it is truly in giving that we receive.

-just as food fuels the body, laughter fuels our soul. So you take more time to laugh and to play.

-just as people grow and change, so it is with love.

-life isn't always fair, you don't always get what you think you deserve; and that sometimes bad things happen to unsuspecting, good people. On these occasions you learn not to personalize things.

-much of the way you view yourself, and the world around you, is a result of all the messages and opinions that have been ingrained into your psyche. You begin to sift thorough all the opinions you've been fed about how you should behave, how you should look, and how much you should weigh; what you should wear and where you should shop, and what you should drive; how and where you should live and what you should do for a living; who you should sleep with; who you should marry and what you should expect of a marriage; the importance of having and raising children or what you owe your parents.

-**negative feelings** such as anger, envy and resentment must be understood and redirected or they will suffocate the life out of you and poison the universe that surrounds you.

-**no one can do it all alone** and that it's OK to risk asking for help.

-**people don't always say what they mean** or mean what they say, and not everyone will always be there for you.

-**principles such as honesty** and integrity are not the outdated ideals of a bygone era, but the mortar that holds together the foundation upon which you must build a life.

-**simple things we take for granted,** things that millions of people upon the earth can only dream about; a full refrigerator, clean running water, a soft warm bed, a long hot shower.

-**the importance of setting boundaries, and learning to say NO.**

-**the only cross to bear** is the one you choose to carry and martyrs get burned at the stake.

-**the only thing you can really count on** is the unexpected.

-**the only thing you must truly fear** is the great fear of all time - FEAR itself.

-**there is power and glory in creating and contributing**; and you stop maneuvering through life merely as a "*consumer*" looking for your next fix.

-**you are foolish for smoking** and destroying your lungs. You stop without complaining. You just do it.

-**you are not going to make everyone happy** and that not everyone will always love, appreciate or approve of who or what you are…and that's OK (they are entitled to their own views and opinions).

-**you deserve to be treated with love,** kindness, sensitivity and respect and you won't settle for less. And, you allow only the hands of a lover who cherishes you to glorify you with his/her touch…and in the process you internalize the meaning of self-respect. Slowly, you begin to take responsibility for yourself by yourself; and you to make yourself a promise to never betray yourself and to never, ever, settle for less than your heart's desire, and you hang a wind chime outside your window so you can listen to the wind. And you make it a point to keep smiling, to keep trusting and to stay open to every wonderful possibility. Finally, with courage in your heart and with God by your side, you take a stand, you take deep breath and you begin to design the life you want to live as best as you can.

-**you don't have the right to demand love** on your terms…just to make you happy.

-**you don't know everything**; it's not your job to save the world…and you can't teach a pig to sing.

-**you must stand on your own,** and take care of yourself; and in the process a sense of safety and security is born of self-reliance.

-**you will never be a size 5 or a perfect 1**; and you stop trying to compete with the image inside your head and agonizing over how you "*stack up*."

-**you will not be more beautiful,** more intelligent, more lovable or important because of the man or woman on your arm or the child that bears your name.

-**your body is your temple and you begin to care for it and treat it with respect.** You begin by eating a balanced diet, drinking more water and taking more time to exercise.

-you awake to all of your possibilities and you begin to look for opportunities.

-you stop trying to control people, situations and outcomes.

-you come to terms with the fact that he is not Prince Charming and you are not Cinderella and that in the real world there aren't always fairy tale endings (or beginnings for that matter) and that any guarantee of *"happily ever after"* must begin with you and in the process a sense of serenity is born of acceptance.

-you stop blaming other people for the things they did to you (or didn't do).

-you stop judging and pointing fingers…and you begin to accept people as they are, and to overlook their shortcomings and human frailties; and in the process a sense of peace and contentment is born of forgiveness.

-you quit making excuses and instead replace them with reasons.

The moral of the story:

Begin to live.

THE BRIDGE BUILDER

An old man going down a lone highway
Came in the evening cold and gray
To a chasm vast and deep and wide
Through which was flowing a sullen tide.
The old man crossed in the twilight dim;
That swollen stream held no fears for him.
But he turned when safe on the other side
And built a bridge to span the tide.

"*Old man,*" said a fellow pilgrim near,
"*You are wasting your strength with building here;*
Your journey will end with the ending day;
You never again must pass this way;
You have crossed the chasm deep and wide-
Why build you this bridge at the eventide?"

The builder lifted his old gray head.
"*Good friend, in the path I have come,*" he said,
"*There followeth after me today*
A youth whose feet must pass this way.
This swollen stream which was naught to me
To that fair-haired youth may a pitfall be;
He, too, must cross the twilight dim;
Good friend, I am building the bridge for him."

THE BUILDING OF A RAILWAY BRIDGE OF LIFE

Compare the *Rhino Spirit* to the building of a bridge? A railway bridge? Yes, when a bridge is built across a river and you leave out a center section, the train is going to go right smack into the river no matter how well all the rest of the span is built. This can be compared to all the tools and systems that, in going to the top, we need to build a solid, permanent, cohesive, and long-term, results-achieving life. If you don't get from one side of the river to the other, whatever the reason, it doesn't make any difference how good some parts of the bridge are. The tools can be world class and still be useless. The best tools in the world, if they do not fit into a system and if people are not taught how to use those tools, are essentially useless.

What does having the *Rhino Spirit* have to do with bridges and trains? As a Rhino, you are the train. The locomotive. You are responsible for pulling the rest of the train. You are pulling, much of the time, not just leading by brute force. Rhinos have the ability to move (or motivate) the rest of the train and in the process gain great momentum. Rhinos teach people how to build their own bridges so that the train can continue on its course. The reason Rhinos seem to work so easily is that they do not use brute force unless they must take a stand for a value or principle. They may have, early in their careers, attempted to lead by brute force, but they quickly learned that they burned themselves out if they continued on that path.

Some people run around trying to figure out what to do first, totally unaware that their fundamental need, in the beginning, should have been to sit down and draw up a plan. Instead, they have gone running off and think that taking *"action"* is something that will get them recognition and/or significance. Just because something is easy to do does not make it the smart thing to do. It just makes it easy. And possibly even fun, at least for a while. Taking action and getting no results is silly and counter-productive. If what you are doing is not working, take a moment to stop and look at what you are doing and, if necessary, find another path. Surely there is a road map to follow. Just keep building relationships, like building bridges.

The moral of the story:

You have to build the whole bridge to make it work. Stick around to complete the task. Build relationships, help people get what they want and you will get everything you ever dreamed of!

PRESS ON.
OBSTACLES ARE SELDOM THE SAME SIZE TOMORROW AS THEY ARE TODAY.

COULD I?

"Could I dream a vivid dream?
Where everything in my life
Is laced with success and happiness.
Forbidden are worries and strife.
Could I see each day as a wonder
Whatever the season may be?
Could I lift my head in the rain, and smile,
And think, "its nature," and its manifold beauty?
Could I really be all I wish for?
The happiest, most successful, the best?
Will I fail to rise to the challenge?
Could I put my deepest desires to the test?
Could I leave someone feeling happier,
Whom I spoke to, or smiled at as we passed?
Could I mould my character to virtue?
An identity that forever would last?
Could I react placidly,
To attitudes blinkered with hate?
Could I endeavor to appreciate the lives and woes,
And the troubles amassed on their plates?
The answer is yes to all the above,
The choice is simply ours to see.
We must strive to learn the power of the Ideal
WE CAN CHOOSE....who we wish to be."

-David Hindmarsh

PILGRIMS CREED

"Don't worry if things seen to run a little slow,
On your journey of life you'll come to know,
Your passions, ambitions, desires and dreams,
Will grace you constantly, as your character weans.
From habits of old, memories of past,
New thoughts come forth, to build on, to last.
Just ask yourself where you want to be,
where do my dreams lie? Look hard and you'll see.
You must keep on plodding, don't forget along the way,
it's not what the day brings to you that counts;
It's quite simply what you do with today!"
-David Hindmarsh

Ignite your passion for life!
Have the fire of desire!

THE COMFORT ZONE

I used to have a Comfort Zone where
I knew I couldn't fail.
The same four walls of busy work
were really more like jail.
I longed so much to do the
things I'd never done before.
But I stayed inside my Comfort Zone,
and paced the same old floor. I said it didn't matter,
that I wasn't doing much. I said I didn't care for things
like diamonds, furs and such.
I claimed to be so busy, with the things inside my
zone. But deep inside I longed for something special of
my own. I couldn't let my life go by, just watching
others win. I held my breath and stepped outside to
let the change begin.
I took a step and with new strength, I'd never felt
before, I kissed my Comfort Zone "*goodbye*"
and closed and locked the door.
If you are in a Comfort Zone, afraid to venture out,
Remember that all winners were
at one time filled with doubt.
A step or two and words of praise,
can make your dreams come true.
Greet your future with a smile;
success is there for you!

THE CRITIC

"It is not the critic who counts, not the man who points out how the strong man stumbles or where the doer of deeds could have done them better. The credit belongs to the man who is actually in the arena, whose face is marred by dust and sweat and blood, who strives valiantly, who errs and comes short again and again because there is no effort without error and shortcomings, who knows the great devotion, who spends himself in a worthy cause, who at the best knows in the end the high achievement of triumph and who at worst, if he fails while daring greatly, knows his place shall never be with those timid and cold souls who know neither victory nor defeat."

-Theodore Roosevelt

SETBACKS PAVE THE WAY FOR MAJOR COMEBACKS

THE EAGLE & THE OYSTER

Once there were two eggs discussing what they wanted to be when they hatched. The first egg said, *"I want to be an oyster when I hatch. An oyster just lies in the water. It has no decisions to make. The currents of the ocean move it about so it doesn't have to plan. The ocean water that passes by is its food. Whatever the ocean provides is what the oyster may receive. No more, no less. That's the life for me. It may be limited, but there are no decisions, no responsibilities, just a plain existence controlled by the ocean."*

Well, the second egg said, *"That's not the life for me. I wish to be an eagle. An eagle is free to go where he wants to go and does as he pleases. Sure, he is responsible for hunting his own food and making survival decisions, but he is free to fly as high as the mountains. The eagle is in control. Not controlled by others. I wish no limits placed on me. I do not wish to be a slave of the ocean. For this I am willing to pay the effort required to live the life of an eagle."*

Which would you rather be? An eagle or an oyster? If you are in a rut, complacent and just existing and are unhappy with the crumbs others throw your way, stop in life right this moment and re-evaluate what you will settle for the rest of your life. Why not instead get the spirit of the Rhino and start all over again? It's never too soon to try again.

MR. H.L. METCHAN

Mr. H. L. Metchan was the editor of the American Mercury Magazine. One day in his normally very noisy newsroom, he shouted out at the top of his lungs, "*It's coming in under the doors!*" Of course, everyone stopped and looked under the doors. "*It's coming up to the bottom of the desk! It's coming up to the seats of our chairs,*" he said as he jumped on the top of his chair! "*What are you talking about?*" the people asked as they could see nothing. And he yelled again, "*It's up to the top of our desks!*" and he jumped on top of his desk! People kept saying, "*What are you talking about?*" And he was on top of his desk, and he said, "*Mediocrity! We're drowning in a sea of mediocrity!*"

Are you surrounded by mediocrity? Do you want to stay average, or do you want to be a high achiever, a champion? Look around. You'll see that very few people will do what it takes to become champions. So many people start something, have high goals, and then when the going gets tough, they quit or start making excuses. Not the person with the *Rhino Spirit*, they have reasons why they succeeded.

The "I've Got It" Must never catch up with the "I Want It."

THE TOUCH OF THE MASTER'S HAND

"T'was battered and scarred, and the auctioneer thought it scarcely worth his while to waste much time on the old violin, but held it with a smile; "What am I bidden, good folks," he cried, "Who'll start the bidding for me?" "A dollar, a dollar"; then, "Two! Only two? Two dollars, and who'll make it three? Three dollars, once three dollars, twice; Going for three..." but No. From the back of the room, a gray-haired man came forward and picked up the bow; then, wiping the dust from the old violin, and tightening the lose strings, he played a melody pure and sweet as a caroling angel sings. The music ceased, and the auctioneer, with a voice that was quiet and low, said: "What am I bid for the old violin?" And then held it up with the bow. "A thousand dollars, and who'll make it two? Two thousand! And who'll make it three? Three thousand, once, three thousand, twice, and going, and gone," said he. Some people cheered, but some of them cried, "We do not quite understand what changed its worth?" Swift came the reply; "The touch of a Master's hand." And many a man with life out of tune, and battered and scarred with sin, is auctioned cheap to the thoughtless crowd, much like the old violin. A "mess of pottage, a glass of wine" a game—-and he travels on. He is "going" once, and "going" twice, He's "going and almost gone." But the Master comes, and the foolish crowd, never can quite understand the worth of a soul and the change that's wrought. . . .**by the touch of the Master's hand."**

-Myra Brooks Welch

THE WISE MAN NEVER CEASES TO WONDER

Here is an important distinction that many people overlook: God made the world; but He does not make your world. He provides the raw materials, and out of them every man selects what he wants and builds an individual world for himself. The fool looks over the wealth of material provided, and selects a few plates of ham and eggs, a few pairs of trousers, a few dollar bills and is satisfied.

*"The wise man builds his world out of wonderful sunsets, and thrilling experiences and the song of the stars, and the romance and miracles. Nothing wonderful ever happens in the life of a fool, an electric light is simply an electric light; a telephone is only a telephone— nothing unusual at all. But **the wise man never ceases to wonder** how a tiny speck of seed, apparently dead and buried, can produce a beautiful yellow flower. He never lifts a telephone receiver or switches on an electric light without a certain feeling of awe."*

-Bruce Barton

THE SONS OF WILLIAM THE CONQUEROR

William the Conqueror was once a great king of England and he had three sons. One day he was in deep thought; and called for his wise men to come into his chambers. They asked him what was the matter. He answered: "*I am thinking of what my sons may do after I am dead. For, unless they are wise and strong and fine leaders, they cannot keep the kingdom, which I have fought and won for them. I am at a loss to know which one of the three ought to be the king when I am gone.*"

The wise men pondered his statement and debated among themselves and finally answered him: "*Oh king! If we only knew what things your sons admire the most, we might then be able to tell what kind of men they will be. Perhaps, by asking each one of them a few questions, we can find out which one of them will be best fitted to rule in your place.*" "*The plan is well worth trying, at least,*" said the king. "*Have each of my sons come before you, and then ask them what you please so you can gather information for me.*"

The wise men talked with one another for a little while, and then agreed that the young princes should be brought in, one at a time, and that the same questions should be put to each. The first who entered the room was Robert. He was a tall, big and was nicknamed Short Stocking. "*Fair Prince,*" said one of the wise men, "*answer me this question: If, instead of being a boy, if you should have been a bird, what kind of a bird would you rather be?*" "*A hawk,*" answered Robert. "*I would rather be a hawk, for no other bird reminds one so much of a bold and gallant knight.*"

Next entered William, his father's namesake and favorite son. His face was jolly and round, had red hair and was nicknamed Rufus, or the Red. *"Fair Prince,"* said the wise man, *"answer me this question: If, instead of being a boy, if you should have been a bird, what kind of a bird would you rather be?"* *"An eagle,"* answered William. *"I would rather be an eagle, because it is strong and brave. It soars above all the other birds. You can't find them very often, they are rare, it is feared by all other birds, and is therefore the king of them all."*

Lastly came the youngest brother, Henry, with quiet steps and a sober, thoughtful look. He had been taught to read and write, and was nicknamed the Handsome Scholar. *"Fair Prince,"* said the wise man, *"answer me this question: If, instead of being a boy, if you should have been a bird, what kind of a bird would you rather be?"* *"A starling,"* said Henry. *"I would rather be a starling, because it is good-mannered and kind and a joy to every one who sees it, and it never tries to rob or abuse its neighbor."*

Then the wise men talked with one another for a short time, and when they had agreed among themselves, they spoke to the king. *"We talked to all three of your sons,"* said the wise men, *"and we have found that your eldest son, Robert, will be bold and gallant. He will do some great deeds, and make a name for himself; but in the end he will be overcome by his foes, and will die in prison."* *"William, will be as brave and strong as the eagle but he will be feared and hated for his cruel deeds. He will lead a wicked life, and will die a shameful death." Henry, will be wise and prudent and peaceful. He will go to war only when he is forced to do so by his enemies. He will be loved at home, and respected abroad; and he will die in peace after having gained great possessions."*

Years passed by, and the three boys had grown up to be men. King William lay upon his death-bed, and again he thought of what would become of his sons when he was gone. He remembered what the wise men had told him; and so he declared that Robert should have the lands, which he held in France, that William should be the King of England, and that Henry should have no land at all, but only a chest of gold.

So it happened in the end very much as the wise men had foretold. Robert was bold and reckless, like the hawk, which he so much admired. He lost all the lands that his father had left him, and was at last shut up in prison, where he was kept until he died. William was so overbearing and cruel that he was feared and hated by all his people. He led a wicked life, and was killed by one of his own men while hunting in the forest. Henry, had not only the chest of gold for his own, but he became by and by the King of England and the ruler of all the lands that his father had had in France.

The moral of the story:

Be the best you can be, you never know who has plans for your future.

THE FIRST DAY OF THE REST OF MY LIFE

This is the beginning of a new day.
I can waste it ... or use it for good.
But what I do today is important,
Because I am exchanging a day of my life for it.
When tomorrow comes, this day will be gone forever,
Leaving in it's place something that I have traded for it.
I want it to be gain and not loss, good and not evil,
Success and not failure, in order that I not regret the
price I have paid for it.
I will give 100% of myself just for today, for you
never fail until you stop trying. I will be the kind of
person I have always wanted to be ...
I have been given this day to use as I will.
Make forgiveness a priority.

DON'T SOIL YOUR HANDS BY SLINGING MUD

WHAT IS YOUR TIME WORTH?

Research shows that the average 70 year old will have spent his life in this manner.
24 years in sleep.
14 years in work.
8 years in amusement.
6 years in education.
6 years eating.
5 years in transportation.
4 years in conversation.
3 years in reading.
8 months in church and prayer.

Use your time wisely!
Be unstoppable!
Achieve your goal!

Why not you and why not now?

DON'T JUST BE BUSY

BEING BUSY- MAKE

YOUR TIME COUNT

HAVE THE RHINO SPIRIT THE REST OF YOUR LIFE!
CHARGE ON THROUGH CHALLENGES,
LEAD THE WAY.

OH LORD,
HELP MY
WORDS TO BE
GRACIOUS
AND TENDER
TODAY, FOR
TOMORROW
I MAY HAVE
TO EAT
THEM.

LISTEN TODAY

Take a moment to listen today to all that your children, little or tall, are trying to say; listen today, whatever you do because someday you will want them to listen to you. Listen to their challenges, and listen for their needs. Praise and recognize their smallest triumphs, and praise their smallest deeds; tolerate their chatter, amplify their laughter, find out what's the matter, find out what they are really after. Tell them that you love them, every single night. And though you might have to scold them, be sure you hold them tight. Tell them often,

"Everything is all right; tomorrow is looking bright!"

Take a moment to listen today to what your children are trying to say; listen carefully today, whatever you do and they will come to you later in life to listen to you!

WE SOW

We sow our thoughts and we reap our actions.

We sow our actions and we reap our habits.

We sow our habits and we reap our character.

We sow our character and we reap our destiny.

THE LAW OF VACUUM

This is a fundamental law of physics. It states that nature cannot tolerate a vacuum. Whenever a vacuum is created, something else will immediately fill the void. If you move an object on your desktop, air rushes in to fill the space that was created. When you move around through space you force the air around you to move too. The same principle applies to the laws of prosperity.

If you remove all the old unwanted things in your life, the universe will quickly try to fill in the space with something else. This is why it is so important to be clear about what you want. If you are not, you'll just get more of the same of what life is bringing you now. Put the Law of Vacuum to work in your life now. Get rid of the old and make room for the new. Clean out your closets and get rid of all the old things that do not reflect the new you. Make a list of what you want to replace these things with. It's a lot of fun and is a real test of faith.

The moral of the story:

Give up old, toxic relationships; those negative people who hold you back. Give them one last opportunity to be positive when they are with you and if they aren't, let them go. As you get rid of what you don't want, watch the universe go to work. It will start to fill up the space immediately. The Law of Vacuum is a definite principle of the planet and you will love taking advantage of it as soon as you realize the truth of how it works.

THE "F" FACTOR

So many times we miss part of life because we don't pay attention to what is right in front of us. Here is an example of just paying attention and focusing: Read this sentence:

FINISHED FILES ARE THE RESULTS OF YEARS OF SCIENTIFIC STUDY COMBINED WITH THE EXPERIENCE OF YEARS.

Now count aloud the "F's in that sentence. Count them ONLY ONCE: do not go back and count them again.

Answer:
There are 6 "F's" in the sentence. There is no catch. Many people don't see the "of's." The human brain tends to see them as V's and not F's. It fools almost everyone.

The moral of the story:
Pay attention to detail.

"Work from 8 to faint."
-Jeff Roberti

THE ANT PHILOSOPHY

Study ants. They have an amazing 4-part philosophy, Here is the first part: ants never quit. If they're headed somewhere and you try to stop them; they'll look for another way. They'll climb over, they'll climb under, they'll climb around. They keep looking for another way. What a neat philosophy, to never quit looking for a way to get where you're supposed to go. Second, ants think winter all summer. That's an important perspective.You can't be so naive as to think summer will last forever. So ants are gathering in their winter food in the middle of summer. An ancient story says, *"Don't build your house on the sand in the summer."* Why do we need that advice? Because it is important to be realistic. In the summer, you've got to think store. You've got to think rocks as you enjoy the sand and sun. Think ahead. The third part of the ant philosophy is that ants think summer all winter. That is so important. During the winter, ants remind themselves, *"This won't last long; we'll soon be out of here."* The first warm day, the ants are out. If it turns cold again, they'll dive back down, but then they come out the first warm day. They can't wait to get out. Here's the last part: How much will an ant gather during the summer to prepare for the winter? All that he possibly can. What an incredible philosophy, the *"all-that-you-possibly-can"* philosophy. What a great seminar to attend - the ant seminar.

The moral of the story:
Never give up, look ahead, stay positive. Study ants.

THE CHALLENGE

"LET OTHERS LEAD
SMALL LIVES,
BUT NOT YOU.
LET OTHERS ARGUE
OVER SMALL THINGS,
BUT NOT YOU.
LET OTHERS CRY
OVER SMALL HURTS,
BUT NOT YOU.
LET OTHERS LEAVE
THEIR FUTURE IN
SOMEONE ELSE'S
HANDS,
BUT NOT YOU."

- Jim Rohn

I MUST BE MYSELF

I have the courage to:
Acknowledge that I have emotional and human rights.
Ask for help and support when I need it.
Be totally honest with myself.
Bless and release toxic relationships from my life.
Break free from the super woman trap.
Celebrate the difference between men and women.
Charge ahead in life.
Choose what is right for me.
Communicate lovingly with understanding as my goal.
Complete unfinished business.
Correct beliefs and assumptions that are incorrect.
Develop healthy relationships.
Embrace my strengths, get excited about life.
Enjoy giving and receiving love.
Face and transform my fears.
Feel all my feelings and act on them accordingly.
Fill my own cup first then nourish others from the
overflow; to continue to press on and go for greatness.
Grant myself permission to play.
Grow through challenges; Have realistic expectations.
Heal old and current wounds if possible.
Insist on being paid fairly for what I do.
Know that I am totally lovable; Make forgiveness a
priority.
Nurture others only because I want to, not because I
have to overcome my addiction to approval.
Own my own excellence.
Plan for the future but live in the present.
Quit feeling responsible for everyone's success.
Respect my vulnerabilities; Say goodbye to guilt.
Set limits and boundaries and stick to them.
Take risks and to accept change in my life.

Love the little child within me.
Plant good seeds in my mind, not weed seeds.
Not settle for anything less than the best life has to offer.
Have skin as thick as the Rhino.
Talk as nicely to myself as I do others.
Throw off the chains of limiting beliefs.
Throw out the clutter of life.
Treat myself with respect and expect others to do the same.
Trust myself.
Value my intuition and wisdom.
Say *"yes"* only when I really mean it.

THE IDEA BANK

The minds potential for thinking and creativity are limitless. We are walking storehouses for facts and experiences, and these impressions in our minds combine in an endless variety of ways to provide opportunities for creativity. A great idea, grabbed firmly at the right moment, and turned into forceful positive action, can change the course of your life forever. Many times ideas are like little jolts of electricity. Catch them when they happen and do not let them slip away into the maze of memories, never to be recaptured. Here is how, jot it down! Use ideas banks to deposit your flashes of inspiration as they occur. Carry them with you for you never know when an idea may strike.

THE EIGHT WINDS

The ancient Chinese know that there are eight winds that move the human spirit. We are all affected by the eight winds:

Praise and Blame

Fame and Defame

Gain and Loss

Joy and Sorrow

On one side, when you succeed, four winds (praise, fame, gain and joy) will be blowing your way. When you fail, it's only natural that the other four winds (blame, defame, loss and sorrow) will be blowing upon you. It is easy enough to be pleasant, when life flows along like a song, but the person who is worthwhile is the one who will smile when everything goes dead wrong.

The moral of the story:
Have the Rhino Spirit to weather whatever situations or challenges enter your life.

It takes guts to leave the ruts!

Have the Rhino Spirit!
THE RHINO DOESN'T GIVE IN OR GIVE UP

Advice from the Rhino:

See no evil

Speak no evil

Hear no evil

"IT'S A FUNNY THING ABOUT LIFE; IF YOU REFUSE TO ACCEPT ANYTHING BUT THE BEST, YOU VERY OFTEN GET IT."

-Somerset Maugham

THE EMPEROR MOTH

The Emperor Moth is the most beautiful, majestic species among all the moths on earth. It has wingspans that are so wide and beautiful when it flies. Prior to it becoming a moth, it must be a pupa in a cocoon. The neck of the cocoon is extremely narrow. For the pupa to become a moth, it must "*squeeze*" itself out of the narrow neck. One day, while watching a pupa struggle, a man was watching from his office window and felt sorry for the moth going through the violent struggle of getting out of the cocoon. The man decided to help it with its struggle and used a pocketknife to widen the neck so that the larva could come out easier. The larva then burst out without going through the entire process of the struggle. But the poor moth dropped to the ground, unable to fly. It could only crawl on the ground instead of soaring through the air with its majestic wings. For the moth to fly, it has to undergo the entire process because as it struggles the fluid to fly is being pumped into the veins of the wings making it able to fly when it completes the struggle. So as it is in life, there are struggles to go through; the heartaches, pains, roadblocks and critics all there to help you become great.

The moral of the story:

When you are upset with situations that are uncomfortable, welcome them as part of your struggle. They are there for a purpose. And let others struggle through their own situations and be very careful not to help them when in fact, they are in the process of becoming great.

THE ROSE

"Some say love,
it is a river that drowns the tender reed.
Some say love, it is a razor that
leaves your heart to bleed.
Some say love,
it is a hunger, an endless, aching need;
I say love it is a flower, and you its only seed.
It's the heart afraid of breaking
that never learns to dance.
It's the dream afraid of waking
that never takes the chance.
It's the one who won't be taken,
who cannot seem to give;
And the soul afraid of dying, that never learns to live.
When the night has been too lonely, and
the road has been too long,
And you think that love is only
for the lucky and the strong,
just remember, the winter,
far beneath the bitter snows,
lies the seed that with the sun's love
In the spring, becomes the rose."
-Amanda McBroo

THE MAN IN THE GLASS

When you get what you want in your struggle for self
And the world makes you king for a day,
Just go to the mirror and look at yourself
And see what that man has to say.
For it isn't your father or mother or wife
Whose judgment upon you must pass.
The fellow whose verdict counts most in your life
Is the one staring back from the glass.
You may be like Jack Horner and chisel a plum
And think you're a wonderful guy.
But the man in the glass says you're only a bum
If you can't look him straight in the eye.
He's the fellow to please, never mind all the rest,
For he's with you clear to the end.
And you've passed your most dangerous, difficult test
If the man in the glass is your friend.
You may fool the whole world down
the pathway of years
And get pats on your back as you pass.
But your final reward will be heartache and tears
If you've cheated the man in the glass.

BE TRUE TO THYSELF

THE VILLAGE GREETER

Back in the time of William Penn, there were many Quaker villages in what is now Pennsylvania. In the center of each of these small villages was a well where people congregated and where strangers were met when they first arrived. One villager, usually an older man, was given the job of Village Greeter. Every visitor would always ask him the same questions:

"What are the people like in this village?"

His job was to ask in return,

"What were the people like where you came from?"

If the strangers replied that the people where they came from were sullen, unhappy, not very friendly or open, then the Greeter would say,

"They are the same here."

If the strangers replied that the people where they came from were warm and happy, open, nice people who cared about each other and made friends easily, then he would say,

"They are the same here."

FROM A TINY SPARK MAY BURST A MIGHTY FLAME

THE FROG STORY

Some frogs were hopping along through the bush in Africa when several of them fell into a deep, dark and murky pit. All the other frogs gathered around the pit and were frantic because they could not reach their frog friends to help them out of the pit. The poor frogs in the pit were jumping with all of their might to get out of the pit. The frogs who were gathered around the pit began to yell at their frog friends to give up because there was no hope that any of them could jump out of the pit. One by one, the little frogs began to give up and flip over, dead. But one little frog kept leaping and leaping and jumping and jumping, with all the energy he could muster. All of a sudden on one of the jumps, he jumped out of the pit and lay exhausted upon the ground. All of the frog's friends surrounded him and were clapping and cheering outrageously. They kept asking him how he did it, why he didn't give up like all of the other frogs had. He had become somewhat of a frog-hero. They said *"Didn't you hear us yell at you to give up? Why didn't you give up like the others?"* Finally, the frog caught his breath and sat up and said *"Ey? I am nearly deaf, I though you were all cheering me on to keep jumping until I got out of the pit. I only kept jumping because I thought you were cheering me on and did not want me to give up!"*

The moral of the story:

Encourage people to not give up. Give people a reason to keep on pressing forward in life. Turn a deaf ear to those who discourage you. Watch your words. Be the one to cheer others on!

THE TRUTH ABOUT GEESE

Have you ever wondered why geese fly in a "V" formation? Here are some interesting facts about why they fly that way.

Fact: As each bird flaps its wings, it creates uplift for the bird immediately following. By flying in a "V" formation, the whole flock adds at least 71% greater flying range than if each bird flew on its own.

Truth: People who share a common direction and sense of community can get where they are going quicker and easier because they are traveling on the trust of one another.

Fact: Whenever a goose falls out of formation, it feels the drag and resistance of trying to go it alone and quickly gets back into formation to take advantage of the lifting power of the bird immediately in front.

Truth: There is strength and power and safety in numbers when traveling in the same direction with those with whom we share a common goal.

Fact: When the lead goose gets tired, it rotates back in the "V" formation and another goose leads.

Truth: Each of us needs to take our turn in giving direction for the good of the whole.

Fact: The geese honk from behind to encourage those up front to keep up their speed.

Truth: We all need to be remembered and stimulated with active support and praise.

Fact: When a goose gets sick or is wounded and falls out, two geese fall out of formation and follow it down to help and protect it. They stay with it until the crisis is resolved, and then they launch out on their own or with another formation to catch up with their group.

Truth: We must stand by each other in times of need.

THE HORN OF THE RHINO SPEAKS VOLUMES

DON'T MESS WITH THE RHINO

SNOWBALLS IN JULY

Stanley Arnold was a man with ideas. He was managing one of 15 Pick-N-Pay stores his father owned in Ohio when a blizzard hit the area. No one could get out in the storm and all of the stores were empty. Employees who had reported to work had nothing to do until Arnold came up with his great idea. He had all the employees make snowballs, 7,900 of them! They packed the snowballs into crates and put them in a deep freeze facility. He enquired of the Weather Bureau when would be the hottest day of the year and found out it would be in mid-July. He then went to see Charles Mortimer, president of General Foods in New York. He proposed a joint promotional sale of General Foods newly introduced Birds Eye frozen food. The sale was to be held in mid-July and General Foods would provide prizes. The sale was named "*Blizzard of Values.*" Arnold proposed to give away... *snowballs.* General Foods agreed to the idea and when summer came, the first day that the temperature went over 100 degrees, the sale began. Police were called in to control the crowds. During the 5 days of Pick-N-Pay's "*Blizzard of Values,*" some 40,000 General Foods samples were given away, along with 7,900 snowballs! Thousands of customers were introduced to new products and the food industry discovered what excitement and enthusiasm could do for sales. All this from an idea from an employee who cared.

The moral of the story:
Be creative, your idea might change the world!

STEP UP AND SHAKE IT OFF

There lived an old worn out, exhausted Rhino. One afternoon, the Rhino fell into a deep pit. The natives assumed that the Rhino was dead. Suddenly they heard the Rhino grunting. After assessing the situation the natives sympathized with the Rhino but figured there was no way to help him get out of the pit. They all began to heap dirt into the pit and onto the back of the old Rhino's back to put it out of it's misery. The Rhino realized this and was frantic but began to think quickly. He realized that every time a load of dirt landed on his back he should and would simply **shake it off and step up!** He did this over and over again; each time the dirt hit his back. **Shake it off and step up...shake it if off and step up!** He kept this up and got a vision that he would survive. He knew it. The blows were painful and he was full of stress but he kept right on **shaking it off and stepping up!** It wasn't long before the old Rhino, battered and exhausted, stepped out of the pit! He had survived, just like he knew he would. He did not let all that dirt bury him and make him give up...no, **he shook off the dirt and stepped up.** What seemed like would bury him actually blessed him all because of the manner in which he handled his adversity. That's life. Face challenges and respond to them positively, refuse to give in to panic, bitterness, to critics, to hypocrites, to those who hurt us, disappoint us, or to situations beyond our control, or self-pity . . .

The moral of the story:
The adversities that come along to bury us usually have within them the potential to benefit and bless us!

Have the *Rhino Spirit*,

Step up and Shake it Off!

NEVER GIVE IN
OR GIVE UP!
LIVE ON THE BRIGHT
SIDE OF LIFE!

**WHEN THE GOING
GETS ROUGH
THE RHINO DOESN'T
TAKE IT SO SERIOUSLY**

THE EASY ROADS ARE CROWDED

"The easy roads are crowded
and the level roads are jammed;
The pleasant little river
with drifting folks are crammed.
But off yonder where it's rocky,
where you get the better view,
you will find the ranks are thinning
and the travelers are few.
Where the going's smooth and pleasant
you will always find the throng,
for the man, more's the pity,
seem to like to drift along.
But the steps that call for courage and the task that's
hard to do, in the end result in glory for the never-
wavering few."
-Edgar Guest

If you think you're too small to
make a difference, you've obviously never
been in bed with a mosquito.

Being yourself is a very nice person to be.

We can't graduate in self-motivation.
It's like eating.
We can't graduate in eating.

"IF"

"If you can keep your head when all about you are losing theirs and blaming it on you, if you can trust yourself when all men doubt you, but make allowance for their doubting too; if you can wait and not be tired by waiting, or being lied about, don't deal in lies, or being hated don't give way to hating, and yet don't look too good, nor talk too wise. If you can dream and not make dreams your master; if you can think and not make thoughts your aim; if you can meet with triumph and disaster and treat those two impostors just the same; if you can bear to hear to the truth you've spoken twisted by knaves to make a trap for fools; or watch the things you gave your life to, broken, and stoop and build 'em up with worn-out tools; if you can make one heap of all your winnings and risk it on one turn of pitch and toss, and lose, and start again at your beginnings and never breathe a word about your loss; if you can force your heart and nerve and sinew to serve your turn long after they are gone, and so hold on when there is nothing in you except the will, which says to them: Hold on! If you can talk with crowds and keep your virtue; or walk with Kings nor lose the common touch; if neither foes nor loving friends can hurt you; if all men count with you, but none too much; if you can fill their unforgiving minute with sixty second's worth of distance run, yours is the earth and everything that's in it and which is more,
You'll be a man my son!"

-Rudyard Kipling

FRIENDS SHOULD BE RADICAL, FANATICAL, AND MOST OF ALL MATHEMATICAL

Radical: A friend should be radical; they should love you when you're unlovable, hug you when you're unhuggable, and bear you when you're unbearable.

Fanatical: A friend should be fanatical; they should cheer when the whole world boos, dance when you get good news, and cry when you cry too.

Mathematical: But most of all, a friend should be mathematical; they should multiply the joy, divide the sorrow, subtract the past, and add to tomorrow, calculate the need deep in your heart, and always be bigger than the sum of all their parts.

EVERYBODY, SOMEBODY, ANYBODY, AND NOBODY

There was an important job to be done and Everybody was sure that Somebody would do it. Anybody could have done it, but Nobody did it. Somebody got angry about that, because it was Everybody's job. Everybody thought Anybody could do it, but Nobody realized that Everybody wouldn't do it. It ended up that Everybody blamed Somebody when Nobody did what Anybody could have.

RECIPE FOR A HAPPY LIFE

Take a couple of whole months, and clean them thoroughly of all Bitterness, Rumors, Hate and Jealousy and make them as fresh and as clean as possible. Now cut each month into 28, 30 or 31 different parts. But don't make up the whole batch at once. Instead prepare it One Day At A Time.

Mix well each day:
One part of Faith,
One of Patience,
One of Courage,
One of Work.
Add one part each of:
Hope,
Faithfulness,
Generosity,
Kindness.
Blend with:
One part Prayer,
One part Meditation,
Good Deeds.
Season the whole with:
a dash of Good Spirit,
a sprinkle of Fun,
a pinch of Play,
a cupful of Good Humor.
Next:
Pour all of this into a Vessel Of Love,
Cook thoroughly over Radiant Joy
Garnish with Smiles serve with Quietness,
Unselfishness and Cheerfulness
And you are bound to have a Happy Life.

EMBRACE THE DAY

When a bird sings it's first song, it is perfect. The bird does not improve the song. When the bee creates its delicious honey, it will never improve the honey. However, you as a human being can change, improve, evaluate, measure and grade your presentations and decide to make them better. You have great potential! You have more potential to create, communicate and relate than you ever dreamed possible! Pioneers and living legends have turned impossibilities into possibilities! Most people dream, set goals and then figure out how they will get what they want. Not me. I get up every day and stop and decide what I am going to get accomplished during the day. Have a blank slate in front of you of the day before you. Get up and embrace the day, whatever it may bring. Look at what you can accomplish and what you can be.

The Laws of Prosperity

Clear your mind of negativity.
Forgive yourself for not having faith.
Set new goals.
Work as if it will all turn out as you planned.

™ Proteus Press

THE RHINO SPIRIT CIRCLES THE GLOBE.

The Rhino Spirit

126

T · H · E
BOTTOM
LINE

Have the
Rhino Spirit

About the Author

Jan Ruhe has collected stories for over two decades. She is an author of many best selling books that today are in six different languages. She has a BA in Sociology and is the mother of three grown children. She and her husband Bill reside in Aspen, Colorado, USA when not traveling the world.

To order in quantities or to order Jan Ruhe's other books: go to:
proteuspress@starband.net
or **www.janruhe.com** or call
Proteus Press at **970-927-9380**,
or fax **970-927-0112**.